China Caravans

史

羅

達

(Fred M. Schroder's Chinese calling card.)

CHINA CARAVANS

Including an Exploration of
the Royal Tombs of Xian
and the
Ill-Fated Restoration of
the Last Manchu Emperor to the Dragon Throne

ROBERT EASTON

Introduction by Audrey Topping

An American Adventurer in Old China

Capra Press
Santa Barbara, California

Printed in the United States of America.

For Andy

Some of this material previously appeared in book form under the title GUNS, GOLD AND CARAVANS.

Library of Congress Cataloging in Publication Data

Easton, Robert Olney.
China caravans.

Fred Meyer Schroder's adventures as told
to Robert Easton.
Rev. ed. of: Guns, gold, and caravans.
3. Caravans in China and Mongolia.
Includes index.
1. China—Description and travel—1901-1948.
2. Mongolia—Description and travel.
3. Schroder, Fred Meyer. I. Schroder, Fred
Meyer. II. Title.
DS710.E2 1982 951.04 81-21742
ISBN 0-88496-179-6 AACR2

CAPRA PRESS
Post Office Box 2068
Santa Barbara, California 93120

CONTENTS

ILLUSTRATIONS

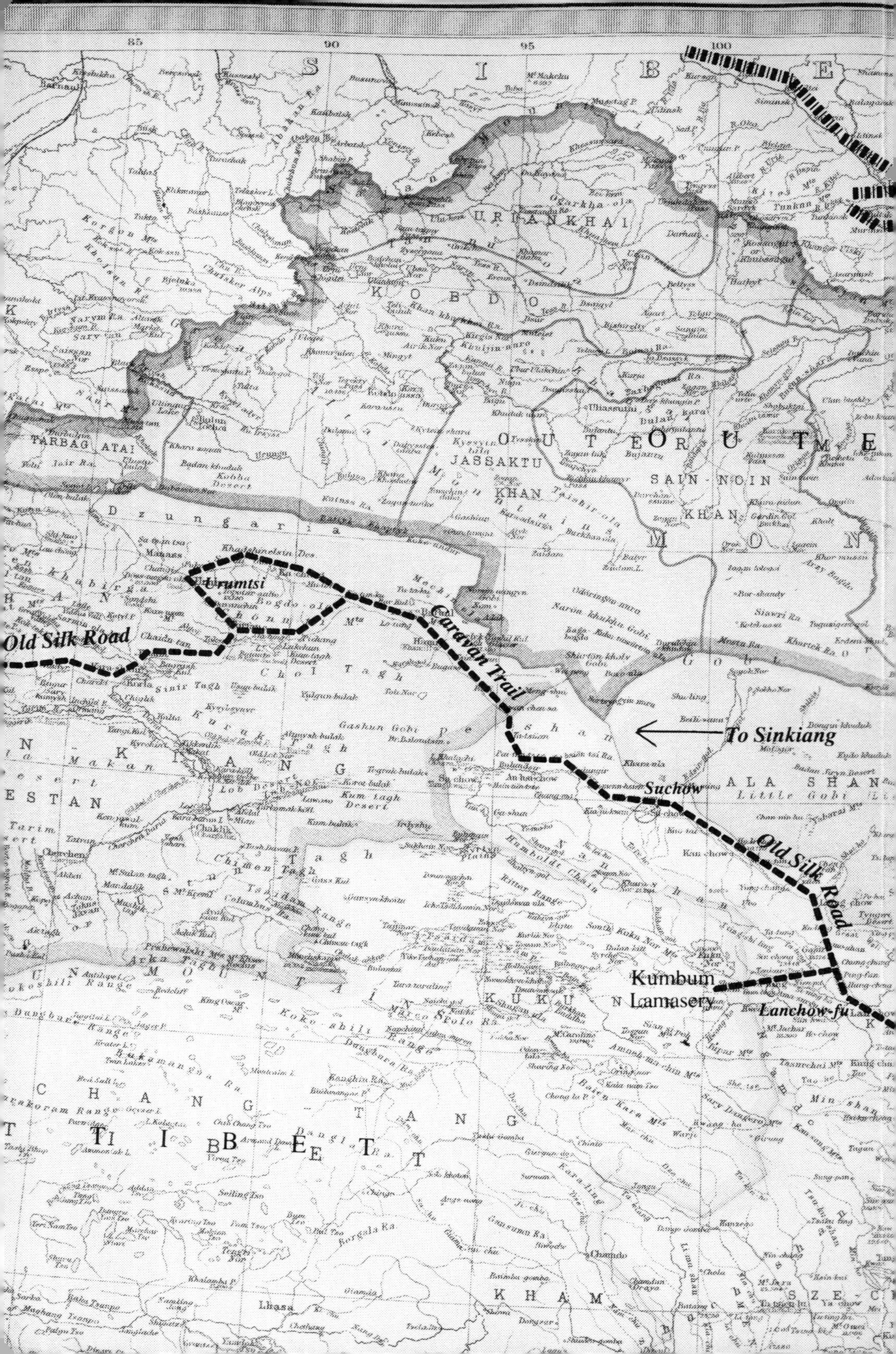

Old Silk Road
Urumtsi
Caravan Trail
To Sinkiang
Suchow
Old Silk Road
Kumbum
Lamasery
Lanchow-fu
URIANKHAI
KOBDO
TARBAGATAI
Dzungaria
JASSAKTU
KHAN
SAIN-NOIN
KHAN
ALA SHAN
Little Gobi
TIBET
KHAM
Lhasa

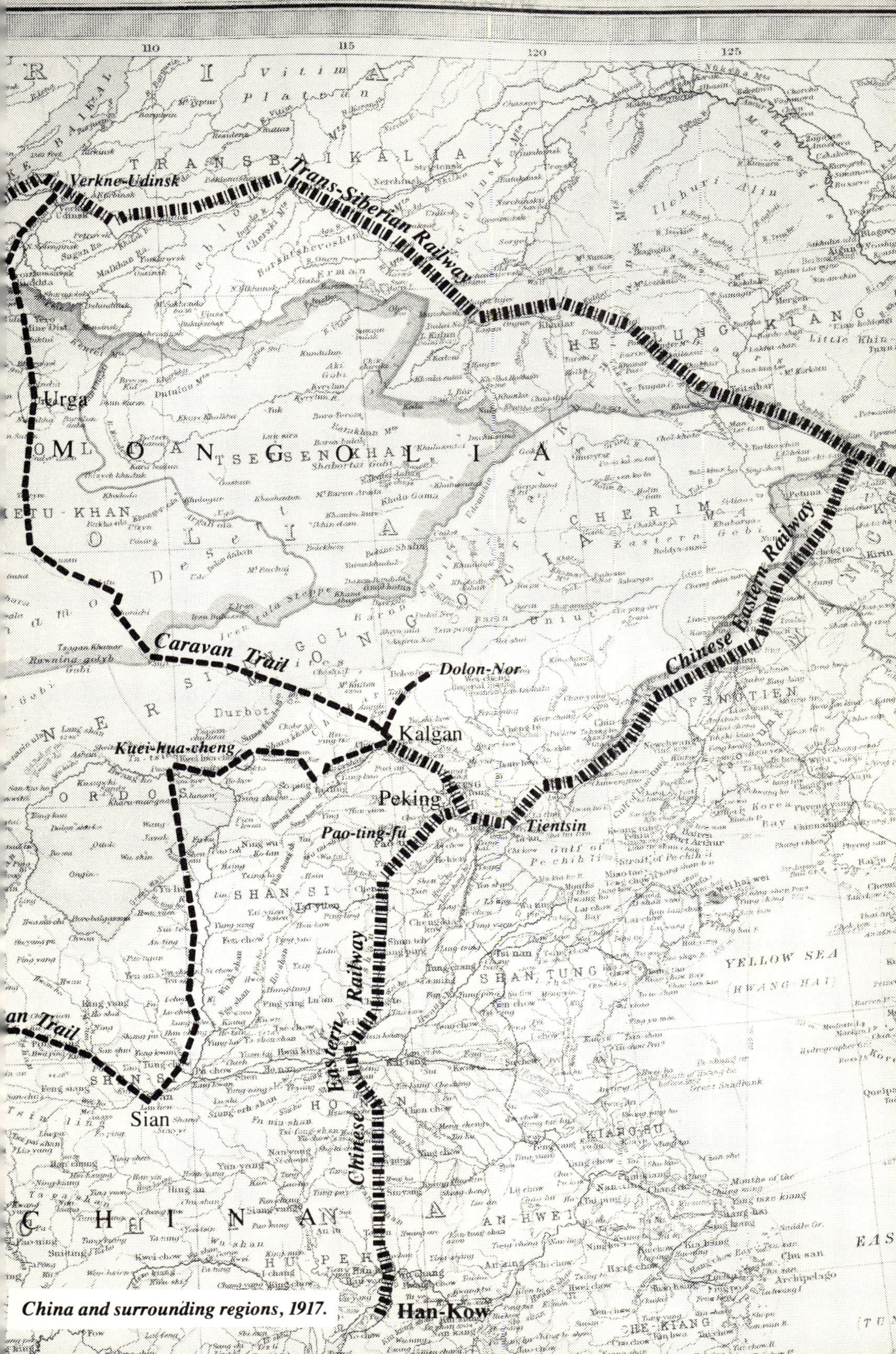

China and surrounding regions, 1917.

Introduction

THERE is an old Chinese saying; "Ch'ien-che shih chien" meaning "The cart ahead is a mirror."

At a time when thousands of American tourists are traveling around the People's Republic of China in the luxury of modern jets, air-conditioned trains and other comfortable conveyances, Robert Easton's dramatic story of an early American adventurer hacking around old China by foot, horseback, camel, houseboat and freight train takes on a new poignancy. Today's travelers can reflect the way it used to be in the hair-raising, often hilarious tales of Fred Meyer Schroder, who roamed China, Tibet and Mongolia during the tumultuous period spanning the downfall of China's 2,200-year-old Imperial Empire and the rise of Sun Yat Sen's Republic.

Most readers will consider themselves fortunate to travel with such ease, but some sensitive souls may suffer an occasional pang of guilt, as I did, because my journey to Tibet was so comfortable compared to Schroder's. From the window of my jet I could see glimpses of a narrow ribbon of road below thrusting steadily onwards, over the barren plateaus, through the precipitous mountain passes and along the banks of the fiercely twisting rivers cascading down from the "Roof of the World." It was along this tortuous route that Schroder rode on his Mongolian horse, accompanied by the Grand Lama of Mongolia who was carried on a regal mule-litter. It took me three and a half easy hours to fly from China's Sinkiang province to Tibet's capital city of Lhasa. It took Schroder over three months to cover approximately the same distance in search of wild licorice and snow leopards. At Tibet's Kumbum Monastery he successfully negotiated with the Tashi Lama to support an ill-fated Mongol revolt against China. In gratitude Schroder gave the Tashi Lama a center-crush Stetson. The Tibetans found the wide-brimmed western cowboy hat so appealing that they copied it in the local felt.

Today, visitors to Tibet often see stylish Tibetans of both sexes wearing western-style cowboy hats at a jaunty angle—a la Schroder.

Schroder brought more than the Stetson to China. He brought the Yankee ingenuity acquired during his youth as a cowboy and horse thief hunter in the "Wild West" and as a gold prospector during the Klondike Rush. This Western cunning not only saved his life on numerous occasions but enabled him to carry on trade in the most improbable places in the Far East. Schroder openly exploited those he could but his earthy good humor and swashbuckling charm endeared him to beggars, thieves and sing-song girls as well as warlords and fallen emperors.

But Schroder's story is more than an adventure, it is history without pain as told by an active participant. Schroder's unique insights into an intermediate moment in China's history are revealing of a China in dissolution, a society that has vanished and can never be seen again. It was during a period when China's economics, moral standards and ancient philosophies were being assaulted and destroyed by the superior armed strength of European powers without and by the sweet smoke of opium and greedy warlords within. Although Schroder was more interested in trade than the analects of Confucius, he was well aware that China's scholarship, art and culture were rooted in the oldest continual civilization in the world and he was constantly searching for traces of its history.

On my last trip to Sian in 1979 I saw the stone tablet commemorating the establishment of Christianity in Sian in 600 A.D. that Schroder looked for but could not find. It now stands in the "Forest of Stone Steles" in Sian's Historical Museum.

The flat-topped pyramids described by Schroder still remain a mystery although it seems highly possible that what he saw was the tomb where China's first sovereign emperor, Ch'in Shih Huang Ti, was buried in 210 B.C. The tomb became world famous some 2,200 years later, in 1974 A.D., when archeologists stumbled upon a huge underground vault about a mile west of the tumulus. The vault contained a whole army of life-size pottery figures. They turned out to be statues of Emperor Ch'in's imperial honor guard consisting of some 7,500 armed warriors, horses and horse-drawn chariots all lined up in battle formation. They had been buried with him to guard him in eternity. It was the beginning of one of the most spectacular excavations of the century.

In 1975 I drove a car over the same territory that Schroder had ridden his horse to visit the Emperor's tomb and see the excavation site. In the middle of a peaceful millet field, the earth had been sharply slashed open and rolled back to reveal a dramatic tableau resembling an ancient battlefield. There, semiburied in the reddish soil of China's Yellow River Valley, were hundreds of battered but beautiful terra-cotta statues of armed warriors, servants and horses pulling manned war chariots. The sight of these powerful figures of men and horses, all life size, reaching out from the rough, wet earth, was unforgettable. Standing in the rain I was moved almost to tears as one is when confronted with great art. Some of the astonishingly realistic figures were still intact and poised as if waiting for a command to attack. Others lay pathetically smashed and scattered. Here and there a hand stretched out of the soil as if asking for help or a booted foot stuck strangely out from the ravaged earth. Helmeted heads, fallen from proud, broken bodies, looked up from their ancient grave with fierce eyes brought glisteningly alive by the rain.

In early 1981, even before the archeologists could release all the soldiers from their cold, turf prison, a new equally amazing discovery was made west of the tomb: two bronze chariots each drawn by four bronze horses and driven by a bronze court official. Unlike the broken pottery army the bronze figures were all intact. The find turned out to be only the tip of the iceberg. In June three more bronze quadrigas were found. All are half life-size. The experts now speculate that the bronze figures may be the vanguard of a voluminous procession, perhaps containing hundreds of bronze horse-drawn chariots bearing realistic and bejewelled statues of the crown prince, the empresses, royal concubines and court officials—all in full regalia. It is a pity that Fred Schroder did not live to see what he had been standing on in Sian.

Many of Schroder's observations have since proved to be remarkably accurate. The legendary "wild hairy man" he described became the subject of a two-year research investigation conducted by the Academy of Sciences in Peking in 1974 and 1975. Scientific workers from several provinces spent over two years combing the least-explored regions of the forests where Schroder used to hunt. More than 100 people, assisted by army volunteers, investigated 600 square miles, covering the area where wild men had been seen.

They found hundreds of people living in or near the forest regions who gave vivid accounts of strange encounters with wild men that fit the description Schroder gave over sixty years ago. Chinese scientists now have two theories about these strange creatures. Some believe the wild men are atavisms—genetic throwbacks to an earlier form of the human species, resulting from chance combinations of ancestral genes. Others say the creatures are actually direct descendants of man's distant ancestor, the great ape.

Although Schroder's China no longer exists, I believe a reading of his adventures will not only entertain, but also add another dimension to present day travels in China. I know it did for me.

—Audrey Topping

China Caravans

1.

Death of Malunga

To the Reader:
Using the first person to capture the voice and idiom of his protagonist, Robert Easton has written a fast moving account of an American adventurer in the thick of events at a critical moment in Chinese history. Fred Meyer Schroder grew up on a California-Mexican border ranch in the 1880s, ran cattle and horses through bandit land, spent his next years in the Yukon during the great Klondike Gold Rush, but it was in China, Mongolia and Tibet that his career came to fruition, and there we begin. The year is 1912.
—*The Publisher*

VIOLENCE or the threat of it underlay our life on the China-Mongolia border as I believe it underlies human experience everywhere. How we meet it may be the central challenge of our existence. We can ignore it, run from it, face it, but the questions it presents are inescapable and in the end personal. What does a man do, for example, when one of his friends murders another?

I first met George Grant when he was introduced to me at the Peking Club by John Fenton of the China Mutual Life Insurance Company. I first met Malunga during a stand-off outside a border village gate.

The two were as different as my friendship for them. Grant, a British subject, civilized, urbane, was Assistant Superintendent of Communications for the Chinese Government. Malunga was a renegade Mongol priest and bandit who preyed on border caravans.

Grant leased a residence from an old Chinese family in the fashionable quarter between the south and east gates of Peking, and there I heard him describe the construction of the newly completed telegraph line linking China to Mongolia which traversed the 900 miles of grassland and desert between Kalgan and Urga. Besides being something of an engineering feat, it had met with a good deal of popular resistance. The grass that fed their flocks and herds was sacred to the nomad Mongols. They considered it sacrilegious to break the surface of the soil even to set the poles for a telegraph line.

Resentment against things emanating from China, as the line did, was strong too.

Chinese settlers pushing outward from the Outer Wall at the rate of eight or ten miles a year were steadily bringing Mongolia under the plow. Their mud-walled villages might be devastated by Mongol raids but rose again as tenaciously as life itself. Finally the Mongols would give in to the extent that they merely levied tribute on the villagers or robbed them at regular intervals instead of trying to annihilate them or drive them back behind the Wall. Chinese encroachment went forward inexorably.

Grant had of course secured approval for his project from the authorities at Urga, the Mongol capital, but though the lama hierarchies were officially against the violence that threatened the line, in practice they did little to control it. Time and again, down came wires and poles. Rank-and-file Mongols enjoyed tying a rope to a pole and watching the line topple over. It wasn't hard to do. The tops of the poles were only nine or ten feet above ground and you could reach them by standing upright in your saddle.

For fun we used to tap the wires and send humorous messages to Kalgan or Urga and we sent some serious ones too, as will be seen.

Reports of increased vandalism against the line had reached me before I left on a business trip to the West. I was out near the Yellow River when I heard the grim news. Grant had sent word to Malunga, a leader in the vandalism, that he could have all the poles and wire he wanted if he would let the line alone. Malunga had no great need for poles or wire. No Mongol did. They built no fences. Such walled compounds as they occasionally used at established camps along the Chinese border, or at Urga—never on the open plains or desert—were built for them by Chinese workers because Mongols disdained to engage in such menial labor. They were horsemen, not workmen. And they just didn't like the telegraph line. Grant finally decided to go and talk to Malunga.

The bandit camp was located within sight of the caravan trail in the region of the Seven Lakes where salt was mined for shipment to Kalgan in oxcarts.

Grant rode out along the trail with a party of maintenance men until he came opposite Malunga's camp. Leaving the rest of the party, he took a personal boy and rode toward the tents while the others watched. Malunga emerged from his yurta accompanied by several of his leaders. Grant dismounted. He and Malunga talked for a few minutes and apparently reached an understanding. Grant turned and walked toward his horse which his boy was holding. Malunga pulled his pistol, a German-made Luger, and fired. Grant fell forward. Then they killed the boy too. The repairmen waiting on the trail hurried to Kalgan and spread the alarm.

This was the news that reached me. Besides horrifying and amazing me it raised certain questions about my own future.

I'd first met Malunga in front of one of those devastated and rebuilt Chinese villages outside the Outer Wall. Jim Brodie and I were approaching it horseback at the head of a train of two-wheeled carts loaded with merchandise to be sold or traded, when a band of about twenty armed men rode over a nearby hill and headed toward us. Jim was my young understudy fresh from Oxford where he had toughened himself in many a rugby scrum.

Removing our rifles from their scabbards and placing them across our saddlebows with muzzles pointing in their general direction, he and I turned to face the approaching strangers while our carts trundled on toward the village gate.

Descending the hill, the band of horsemen disappeared into a watercut two hundred yards from us and did not reappear. This put Brodie and me in the position of having to retreat, deploy and get ready to fight, or stand our ground. We chose to stand, and after a few minutes a solitary figure appeared on our side of the cut and rode slowly toward us.

He was powerfully built, his manner calm and confident. He carried a rifle slung across his back and a pistol in a belt holster. When he'd approached to within a respectful distance, he drew rein and inquired politely if we were trading at this village.

"Yes, we are trading here. And you and your friends—what is your destination?"

He grinned audaciously. "We trade at this village too!"

"No," I said firmly, though I admired his nerve and even sympathized with his desire to make the Chinese pay for their encroachment on Mongol soil, "you are not going to trade at this village. You are going to trade at that one, down the road there," indicating the direction from which we had come. "Your friends watching from the watercut will see your signal. They will meet you down the road. Not here. This is our village."

His smile grew broader while he remained silent a moment or two. "Very well. Perhaps we shall meet again under different circumstances." He bade us goodbye and rode off down the road in leisurely fashion. His friends met him. That was Malunga.

We didn't meet again for nearly a year. Then, outward-bound with a caravan of tea and silk for Urga, I stopped one afternoon near the Seven Lakes. From time to time we'd seen armed men on the promontories and knew bandits were watching us but there had been no attack. Our caravans were manned mostly by Outer Mongols from the high plains toward Urga, as tough fighting men as there are. Our rule-of-thumb used to be: one Inner Mongol from near the Chinese border equals ten Chinese; one Outer Mongol equals five Inner. As further deterrent we were flying the British flag as usual. We never flew the Stars and Stripes. Might as well wave a handkerchief. Nobody knew what they meant. But Malunga, if it was his band, should know better than to meddle with his northern cousins as well as the Union Jack and the British Empire.

Toward sundown his messenger rode into camp. After customary salutations the man handed me a calling card, a strip of red paper bearing three black characters arranged vertically, spelling "Ma-lun-ga." Then he invited me to dine that evening with his master.

I took a boy as Grant was to do later and rode to the camp in the hollow. As I approached through the gathering dusk, Malunga's people assembled to stare at me. I remembered once riding up to such a camp on the high plains and overhearing a ten-year-old boy ask his parents: "Shall I kill him for you?" Malunga emerged from his tent in company with several of his headmen and greeted me cordially with a "God be with you!" which I returned. Following him inside, I left my whip at the door as custom also dictated. Had I carried rifle or pistol I would have left them too, and if I hadn't returned for a month I would probably have found them exactly as I'd left them, such was the sanctity of Mongol hospitality.

He led the way around the left-hand side of the circular felt tent, the male side, toward a low wooden bench where, after much discussion as to who should sit first, we both sat at the same time.

Malunga's wife had put on her elaborate jeweled headdress for the occasion. It was fan-shaped, about twenty inches high, of gold and silver filigree inlaid with precious stones, a crown that made those of most European princesses look paltry. Dignified by it, she served us hot rice wine from a flask kept warm in a brazier of burning camel's dung. And when he had drunk and she had drunk and the headmen and relatives who had crowded into the tent behind us had drunk, we played cards—fan-tan, and the poker the Mongols had learned from us foreign devils (played with the narrow Chinese deck whose face cards had Chinese faces)—and we ate boiled mutton by the light of the argol stoves, and played again and I took care to lose.

He said slyly at last: "You were as good as dead that day we met in front of the village gate!"

"So were you!" I rejoined. We had a good laugh. We understood each other.

On a later occasion he came to my camp, drank my whiskey and smoked my cigarettes; we played cards and I won back most of what I'd lost before. He never troubled my caravans.

Now, however, if he could kill Grant he could kill me. He must be punished for what he had done and for its implications. To survive in hostile surroundings among a population vastly outnumbering us, we foreigners on the border must maintain the illusion of our invincibility or be swept away.

On returning to Kalgan I made inquiries. Malunga had vanished. Chinese soldiers were said to be scouring the countryside for him. His persecutions of the Chinese had given him prestige among Mongols while to the Chinese he was Public Enemy Number One. He was death and destruction to their caravans. His spies informed him, he struck, and there was little left for the wolves and wild dogs. I guessed that the soldiers scouring the countryside weren't scouring too hard, having small taste for the medicine Malunga's band administered. They numbered about forty fighting men. Though not so numerous as some, they were an elite group. A lama led them. Once a lama always a lama, the Mongols believed. And perhaps the gods continued to look with favor upon one who had served their altars and still had the power to do so.

What changed Malunga from priest to renegade I never learned. Even now I could sympathize with his attitude toward the telegraph line. Had it not been for Grant's murder, I would have sympathized more. When I first came to Mongolia you could ride 3,000 miles from Manchuria to Russian Turkestan, as far as across the United States, and never see a piece of plowed ground. Grassland, mountains, deserts lay undisturbed as in the beginning. Grant changed this. He was the forerunner of many such changes. Some premonition may have moved Malunga to raise his hand against Grant. Or perhaps it was pure deviltry. Perhaps elements of racial and religious animosity entered the picture.

This was the bungalow in our compound at Kalgan on the Mongolian border.

I talked to the Chinese police. No word of Malunga from north, south, east, or west. My Mongols, who had their own sources of information, confirmed this. I decided that if he were nowhere else he might be right under our noses in the hundred-mile stretch of mountains lying along the border between Kalgan and Kuei-hua-cheng. But first it was necessary to find Grant's body to provide the evidence of death that would enable his mother back in Scotland to cash his policy with the China Mutual.

Taking one of my best Mongols, Jaw-tor, I rode out the caravan trail toward the Seven Lakes. On the hill beyond Malunga's abandoned campsite was a burial ground. The Mongols did not break soil even for burial. They exposed their dead. Wolves, eagles, vultures, and feral dogs disposed of the remains in short order. Jaw-tor was too superstitious to climb the hill to the cemetery so I went up alone. Its top was strewn with bones, the campsite below having been used since time immemorial. Most of the bones were old. Among the fresh ones I found a skull with gold fillings in its teeth and a bullet hole at its back. No dentist had ever practiced in Mongolia to my knowledge, and when I came across a piece of whipcord trouser bearing the mark of a Peking tailor, I felt I'd found what I was after.

Back in Kalgan we wired the British Ministry that the remains would reach Peking by rail next day, arranged the bones as best we could in a large wooden cigarette case, bored holes and fitted rope handles at its ends, covered the box with crepe and made a double bow of black chiffon. In company with Frans August Larson, our resident trader-missionary, and other friends, we put the box on the train and said goodbye to Grant.

Then I turned my attention to Malunga. I took Jaw-tor who would go with me anywhere except into a graveyard. Wearing native sheepskins, he could if need be mingle with the local population, gather information, summon help. Like most Mongols he had exceptional eyesight and could see as well or better than I. He carried a .303 British Winchester as I did, and his .38 Colt Army. In addition I carried my two .45s from California-Mexican border days, bone-handled, their triggers honed to a quarter-pound pull, and a pair of eight-powered Zeiss field glasses and a sixty-power telescope.

We made up saddle packs of dried antelope, biscuits, bully beef, and some American canned tomatoes. Then we selected two tough ponies and started up the pass into the barren mountains where I guessed Malunga might be hiding. For three weeks we wandered, searching out the land, traveling mostly by night, lying up and watching by day.

We looked for signs of men or stock and smelled for camp smoke that would hang long in those still valleys. A camp of two hundred persons is hard to hide. Counting women, children, and old men, Malunga had what amounted to a village, complete with flocks of sheep and herds of cattle and horses, possibly camels, certainly dogs. What we were searching for would look like a regular Mongol encampment. Or they might see us first and that might end the hunt. There was no question of my coming to pay a social call. Of course they could hold me for ransom, a recognized business practiced by a number of professional bandits.

One morning while scanning a distant peak through my field glasses I saw a black dot among some boulders. It was a man.

With the aid of my telescope I distinguished two more. They were a long way off—five or six miles—and on a ridge higher than ours, but I could see their rifles and bandoliers.

Jaw-tor and I lay still all day and watched. We discovered another lookout post on the same ridge three or four miles beyond the first. At sundown the guards changed. That meant their camp was close by, probably just over the ridge.

I selected a low spot on the ridge midway between the two lookouts, a spot I thought would be hidden from both and yet give us command of the country beyond, and now our really cautious moving began.

Riding was out of the question. Leading a horse enables you to feel your way in the dark and avoid the rocks and pitfalls. A snort or a sneeze could be a major hazard, but there was not much danger of our animals neighing unless they saw other stock. During the day we picketed them with a rope tied from halter to foreleg and remained in a secluded canyon in the shelter of some large boulders near a small spring. When night came we started afoot up the slope toward the low spot on the ridge between the two lookouts. At dawn we lay on the crest.

The first light showed us what we hoped to see—a faint haze of smoke, the smoke made by burning dung when the braziers are first lighted in the morning. At other times dung fires are practically smokeless. Below us lay a hidden valley shaped like a crooked squash. Its neck opened toward the high grassland of the Mongolian Plateau. Its wider part was concealed by foothills and cupped by the mountains to form a natural hideaway. A stream ran through it. Stock grazed in it. Eighteen or twenty tents were pitched beside the stream and the only place you could see it readily was from above as we were doing.

We watched the women go down to the creek for water and the children playing with the dogs. Then the women went with some of the older children and milked the cows and mares before the herds were turned out to graze for the day. The horses were mostly adult stock that could readily be used or sold. Probably most of them had been stolen.

I focused my telescope on what I thought was Malunga's tent. After a while he emerged and greeted three or four boys who were bringing some ponies to water before taking them onto the plain.

Where he performed priestly duties among his people I never

learned. He didn't wear red or sacred medallions, just the ordinary padded sheepskin trousers, coat, and peaked wool hat.

Two groups of horsemen rode off in opposite directions. We guessed they were reliefs for the lookouts. Sure enough, after an hour or so, two similar groups came back.

Malunga talked with his men as they stood watching their women work, smoking their long-stemmed pipes with small brass bowls and a bone mouthpiece resembling those I'd first seen at Indian Point on the Siberian coast when trading there for furs. Some repaired saddles or cleaned rifles, ran footraces or wrestled. Toward noon a fat-tailed sheep was killed for common use and after lunch there was a siesta. Riders came and went—spies perhaps, or messengers.

We studied the lay of the land and the habits of the camp. I sketched a map in my notebook. We took turns sleeping and watching, alert for unusual signs such as a lark rising without singing or a raven swooping low to look at something.

Toward sundown the herds were brought in and the women milked the cows and mares again before dark. The guards on the peaks changed at sunset.

After dark Jaw-tor and I climbed cautiously down to our camp, watered our horses, fed them a handful of grain and changed their picket ground. Then we ate cold dried antelope and canned tomatoes, wrapped ourselves in sheepskins and curled up behind rocks to sleep. At dawn we were at our observation post. Another day's watching confirmed what I'd suspected. The camp was vulnerable to attack from the plain and to a properly led party crossing the ridge at the spot where we lay.

We left the country as cautiously as we'd come into it. I decided not to inform the Chinese authorities. They were too unreliable. This was a job for Mongols. I telegraphed Urga where we maintained a trading compound. Within a few days a detachment of troops met Jaw-tor and me at the first relay station, a mud hut, on the telegraph line.

I briefed the lieutenant in charge. He divided his men into two groups, about thirty in each, he to lead one, I the other. They were the tough Outer Mongols I have described. Five mornings later we would attack the camp, he from the plains side, I from the mountain. I would guide my party along the route Jaw-tor and I had followed. Under cover of darkness we would slip across the ridge between the lookouts. The signal to attack would be a coat waved from the crest of the small hill concealing the camp from the plain, at such time as it was light enough to shoot.

At dawn when the animals are beginning to stir and the smoke is starting to rise from the tents, I lay with my men against the bank of the creek less than two hundred yards from Malunga's camp. We'd crept as close as we dared. Even now the dogs might scent us. Daylight was growing. Soon the herd boys would be coming from the stock and the relief guards saddle up and leave the lookouts.

I kept my eyes fixed on the crest of the hill beyond camp. Malunga should have posted a guard there but evidently felt safe from that side, his Mongol side. In a few minutes I saw the figure of a man rise in silhouette upon the hill and wave a coat. My men and I stood up and walked toward the tents, firing as we went, hearing the simultaneous shots from the hill and seeing the muzzle flashes.

At first there had been no answering fire but now the lead was beginning to sing around us. They nearly equaled us in number and after the first surprise fought back hard. But Malunga's tent remained quiet.

About a hundred yards separated us when he emerged from his doorway. He held his rifle in his hands as I did mine. We saw each other at approximately the same time. He must have realized then who was after him. We started walking toward each other. I watched his hands. If you're too far away to see their eyes, watch their hands. When his started to move, I fired from the ready. He hesitated, then pitched forward on his face. He tried to raise his rifle but couldn't.

When I bent over him I saw my bullet had gone through his belly at the navel and a pool of blood was beginning to form under him and soak into the ground. He looked up at me, defiant, but unable to speak. If there was reason deeper than deviltry for his sabotage of the telegraph line and his wanton destruction of so many Chinese caravans and his murder of Grant, the time was past for his telling it, just as the time was past for my saying I was sorry for what I had done to him. Of all the men I was obliged to deal with violently, none moved me so much as Malunga.

When the lieutenant and his men realized he wasn't going to die immediately, the question of what to do with him arose. He was their official prisoner but they didn't want to be troubled by doctoring him or hauling him all the way to Urga for punishment, assuming he lived till then. But they dared not put an end to him. He was a priest and to touch him with hostile intent would be to incur the wrath of the gods. So they caught a wild horse from his herd, tied him to its tail with some of the wire he'd taken from Grant's telegraph line, and Malunga was dragged to his death.

My life resumed its former channels. The border became a safer place for caravans. Chinese settlement of Inner Mongolia proceeded steadily, despite sporadic Mongol resistance. And the deaths of Grant and Malunga were soon overshadowed by larger and more violent events whose focus was elsewhere but which affected us all.

I take a break between caravan trips.

Street scene, Pao-ting-fu.

2.

China in Revolution

I'D REACHED China from California in 1907 on the Pacific Mail liner "Manchuria." The new land I was stepping into was still the Ancient Cathay of Marco Polo, the Imperial Cathay my colleague there William Ashley Anderson later described as "an empire of walled cities, and mandarins of the seven orders, the Manchus of the Nine Banners, of huge palanquins carried on the shoulders of massed porters, of gold-encrusted and embroidered dragon robes, of men with shaven heads and long queues and women on pinched lily-feet." It was also the China of starving half-naked toiling coolies hitched like work horses to carts piled high with freight or merchandise, while others balancing long poles on their shoulders were nearly hidden by loads suspended at either end, and still others pulled rickshaws carrying people or their belongings. It was also the China of the twentieth century.

The docks along the Shanghai Bund were lined with ships of many nations. Across a broad avenue bordering the waterfront rose a wall of modern-style commercial buildings, clubs, and hotels, and from the deck where I stood I could see trolley cars, bicycles, men wearing business suits and women in smart dresses who might have stepped off the streets of San Francisco or London.

This was also the China of the dominant and often intolerant foreigner. The Bund and everything I was looking at were in Shanghai's Foreign Quarter, where there were signs in the parks prohibiting dogs or Chinese.

The British-American Tobacco Company's headquarters, a four-story brick building, faced the waterfront avenue. A stream of men wearing long blue gowns, their hair in queues down their backs, flowed in and out of it, mingling with those in modern business suits I'd noticed earlier. An Otis elevator made in the U.S.A. lifted me to the top floor.

As I walked along a corridor toward the office of James A. Thomas, British-American Tobacco's Far Eastern manager, I glanced through an open doorway and was astonished to see, sitting at an executive's desk giving dictation to a pretty Chinese secretary, a friend of mine from pioneer Alaska days, Tom Cobbs. "Why Cra—!" I broke out, almost uttering the nickname "Craphouse" by which we'd known Tom at Nome. Tom was a big, boisterous, irrepressible Virginian who'd been among the 20,000 gold-seekers landing on the Nome beach during that memorable summer of 1900. Too late to find a claim, Tom, who was nothing if not enterprising, got a bright idea when he ran foul of the camp law requiring a man to walk a couple of hundred yards beyond the fringes of settlement before relieving himself. He built a rickety pier into Bering Sea, erected privies on it, sold tickets at twenty-five cents each. By the summer's end he was making a small fortune and Tom Cobbs and his tickets were the standing joke of Nome.

He'd recognized me the same instant I'd recognized him and I saw him flush with embarrassment as he heard his nickname half out of my mouth. When his secretary turned to see who'd interrupted them, he raised a finger to his lips and tipped me the wink. I smiled and walked on, feeling myself already at home.

I found J.A. Thomas to be a tall soft-spoken North Carolinian with top-drawer simplicity and good manners. He wore a three-piece suit with a gold watch chain threaded through a vest buttonhole. As a younger man he'd revolutionized the tobacco business in the Orient by asking himself one question: How many cigarettes per package would yield a reasonable profit and still sell for a coin worth about two U.S. cents? After extensive calculations he came up with the answer, five. He took his idea to James B. Duke, his boss in the American Tobacco Company. Amalgamating with British Imperial Tobacco, they built a trading empire in the Far East second only to Standard Oil's; and the Chinese, pipe smokers for hundreds of years, became cigarette smokers.

Though he received an annual salary of sixty thousand from B.A.T., an enormous sum for those days, and had immense power, Thomas was no ruthless exploiter. The Chinese had been growing tobacco for centuries but it was heavy pipe tobacco, not the aromatic variety used in cigarettes. He brought in experts from North Carolina who taught native farmers how to cultivate fine-quality cigarette tobacco. Seed and fertilizer were also imported from the States, and soon Shantung province, the center of the new tobacco culture, became one of the most prosperous in China where before it had been one of the most depressed. Fine tobacco was also grown in Manchuria and many other parts of the country. As the demand increased, Thomas built cigarette factories in China and more jobs and more prosperity were created.

When we'd talked a while and he'd read my letters of introduction, he offered me the job I wanted. As an independent operator, I would receive a small salary from the company but could engage in any business not directly competitive with B.A.T.'s. It sounded good. I wanted freedom to act on my own and see the country and I liked Thomas and the far-flung nature of his operations, which were bound to take me to the frontiers and outdoor life I was used to; and with Cobbs at hand I would be starting among friends. But first I wanted to acquaint myself with the language and customs of China. I told this to Thomas, explaining that I wanted to immerse myself completely in native surroundings without any foreign influence. I argued that I would be of more use to him and to myself in the long run if I could do this now. On the map on the wall he showed me where the railroad ended far up in Anhwei. I asked leave to go there and steep myself in Chinese life. He agreed and I went back down the hall to settle accounts with Cobbs.

At the Long Bar at the Shanghai Club, said to be the longest in the world, Tom and I reached an agreement over gin-tails. I would say nothing about his pierhead privies. But every time I was in Shanghai he would have to buy the drinks. He'd taken his stake made at Nome, invested it in British-American Tobacco, and was now manager of the company's Shanghai office.

He thought my idea of going into the hinterland a crazy one but helped me find the indispensable first ingredient, a good personal boy. Having a good Chinese servant was like having a benevolent genius looking after your needs. With quick alert little Lu to guide me I boarded the train for Nanking. He carried a basket of food and personal belongings in his lap. As we sat opposite each other, he would hold up an object, say its name, and I would repeat after him. By the time we reached Nanking I'd learned how to say "What is that?" From there on, things got easier.

At railhead on the unfinished line running northward toward Tientsin, we got off. I put my finger on the map a substantial distance into the interior and said we would go there. He shrugged. "All right. We go there." I made him understand we would need a cart for our luggage and horses for ourselves. He disappeared but soon returned with some sample carts and their owners. I selected a high-wheeled, cloth-hooded model and left arrangements to him. Next I tried to explain that we would need riding horses. He brought me cart horses and draft horses. Finally I got my saddle out of my dunnage. It was a lightweight California model made to order by the Visalia Stock Saddle Company of San Francisco, California's premier saddlemakers for many years. I held it up and indicated I wanted something to go under it. Lu got the idea but suggested we postpone our purchases. "Horses no good here! Up-country better!"

Up-country we went and in the recesses of Anhwei we stayed five months while I did little but observe, listen, get acquainted with the people and their customs. The language presented no difficulty. I'd been exposed to so many in California, Mexico and Alaska that Chinese was simply one more. I found the people admirable in many ways: intelligent, industrious, and for the most part friendly, though now and then I heard the shrill derisive shout of *yang kwei-tse* (foreign devil) as I passed. They were very tidy in their habits. Shops, houses, and courtyards were swept clean. As summer came on, dust was laid by sprinkling. Every bit of waste was used. Instead of being dumped into rivers or lakes, human excrement was collected and placed on the fields to fertilize crops. Clothes were washed at every pool and stream, the dirt beaten out (as the Indian women of my early California days had beaten it out) because there was no soap. The Chinese had no knowledge of modern hygiene yet blew their noses on bits of paper which they discarded, a hygienic measure we didn't practice till Kleenex came along years later. Having invented paper the Chinese were using toilet paper, too, and paper towels centuries before we did. Even the smallest towns had public hot baths, and the most numerous among a myriad of commercial peddlers and travelers were the street-side barbers who shaved heads and cheeks, trimmed queues or filled them out with pieces of string, cleaned your eyes, ears, and nostrils—using the same cotton swab for all customers!

Opium pills were a standard remedy for most ailments. You could buy a handful from any apothecary. For the more discerning there were the traditional herbs, potions, and acupuncture treatment which, with the antibodies developed in the national bloodstream over the centuries, combined to keep the people surprisingly healthy. There were sufferers from disease, smallpox, leprosy, typhus, yes, but there were few weaklings or mental misfits. Attrition, the inexorable demands of survival, weeded out the unfit.

Both men and women wore long loose jackets of blue cotton or blue or purple silk, fitting closely at the neck, with wide sleeves, and wide short trousers. Hats were of close-fitting silk or wide-brimmed straw. Shoes were commonly of cotton or silk with thick felt soles. Both men and women carried fans, sometimes sticking them at the backs of their necks, as I later learned to do with Mongolian and Tibetan prayer wheels when shooting game for my caravan crews. Both sexes smoked pipes or cigarettes. Both were abstemious in their habits and as a rule modest and decorous in their behavior, though they privately looked down on all foreigners including me.

Every household I visited had a wall niche or shrine where a tablet displayed the family genealogy. Candles burned in front of it, keeping alight symbolically the family's eternal flame of life. Offerings were set out on special occasions. This was the traditional ancestor worship associated with Confucianism but there was little other evidence of religious practice except at funerals and weddings, or in the form of pilgrimages to sacred places. At deeper level, though, there was a primitive superstitious reverence for the forces of nature. *Feng-shui*, this reverence was called, or literally "respect for wind and water"—wind representing the breath of life, water the force that both nurtures and destroyes. *Feng-shui* expressed the precariousness by which we all exist in the face of the forces of creation and destruction, which also move within ourselves.

For entertainment I joined the crowd around the storyteller under the sacred tree or at the village streetcorner, listening to his tales of ancient princes and princesses, dragons and demons. From time to time he accented dramatic moments in his recitation with a sharp *ping* of his tuning fork as Homer did by plucking the strings of his lyre ages earlier. And there were the games: mahjong, go, fan-tan, or the poker which I taught my Chinese friends. They were inveterate gamblers, more so than any people I ever encountered.

Food was plentiful and good. There were thick tasty soups made of birds' nests, ducks' tongues, or chickens' brains, served with toasted unleavened bread. There were game birds such as pheasant and duck, fish dipped in batter and fried whole, morsels of pork simmered in hot fat until deliciously crisp, plus rice and vegetables of many kinds. Eggs were often preserved in a solution of salt, lime, or wood ash and served fresh after months or years of storage. There were always the noodles which Marco Polo brought back to Europe and which evolved into spaghetti. And there was *samshu*, rice wine, served hot in small bowls. Dinners were apt to be incredible events lasting most of the night and including twenty-four, thirty-six or as many as seventy-two courses (always a multiple of four for the four seasons or four directions) depending on the expansiveness of the occasion.

And yet the good nature of the people could be misleading. Underneath lurked a latent violence, ready to break out on provocation. The bloody events of the Boxer Rebellion, the popular uprising against foreigners, were only a few short years away. China had paid dearly for that bitter experience in the form of cash indemnities and economic or territorial concessions to foreign interests. But I remembered Thomas' warning: "Always move boldly. Always exercise authority." Several B.A.T. men had been killed by Chinese mobs which turned suddenly ugly.

Both Thomas and Cobbs were surprised by my familiarity with Chinese life when I returned to Shanghai.

My first assignment took me to Chinkiang, a major port, strategically located for trading purposes at the junction of the historic Grand Canal with the Yangtze River. My partner there was young J.W.G. Brodie, aforementioned, whose family owned a substantial quantity of B.A.T. stock and who later became one of the leading businessmen of Wellington, New Zealand. Brodie and I lived in style in a bungalow formerly occupied by an official of the San Francisco based Matson Steamship Company. It was situated on the crest of a hill overlooking city and river, surrounded by extensive grounds, stables and outbuildings. We had a total of twenty-seven servants to wait on us, and learning to play my role among them as gentleman-master took some study. After years of helping myself, I had to learn how to stand aside and *be* helped.

If I found a bone one of our hunting dogs had left on the lawn, I couldn't pick it up without seriously jeopardizing the order of things. I must call our number-one house boy who in turn called our number-two house boy who in turn called our dog coolie, whose responsibility it was to pick up the bone. Such were the ways of my new world.

If Brodie and I went down the hill into the city, we each had four chair-coolies to carry us. Yet this division of labor was welcomed. It had existed for centuries. In an overpopulated country it provided a maximum of jobs, no matter how meagerly paid, plus a chance for kumshaw, food, housing, status.

At the foot of our hill was a park and tennis club where we occasionally had tea with the gentry from the consulates and their wives and daughters. On more enjoyable occasions we played base-ball or cricket with the crews of the gunboats "Helena" and "Duck", or went hunting in the New Forest three miles away where there were deer and leopard; or we prowled the old trenches, not far beyond, dating to the days of the Taiping Rebellion and the British general, "Chinese" Gordon, who'd commanded Chinese Imperial troops there, aided by an American general named Ward. Together they had put down that earlier uprising against foreigners and Manchu rule. Ward, I disovered, was a young soldier of fortune who'd been hired by wealthy Chinese citizens of Shanghai to protect their city at the head of a polyglot force of Europeans and Spanish Philip-pine mercenaries, and when he was killed in action, Gordon took over. The pattern of Chinese life seemed to be one of continual upheaval with foreigners playing a leading role.

To entertain us at home Brodie and I had our hunting dogs, riding horses and a tame cheetah we used for hunting, and from time to time we gave wild parties, when sing-song girls with their fantastically painted and powdered faces sat on our respective knees and sang to us in their high-pitched off-key voices to the accompaniment of their *hu-hus*. On a hill nearby lived a missionary family who disapproved of our carryings on. Years later when I read her autobiography I learned that it was the family of Pearl Buck.

From Chinkiang we covered a wide trade territory. Traveling in a forty-foot houseboat towed by a motorboat (the houseboat having plenty of room for servants, merchandise, and our native sales crew), we traversed the historic Grand Canal and its tributaries southward toward Suchow and Hanchow or north through the rich coastal lowlands toward Peking. Parts of the canal had been built as early as 400 B.C., and it had once been the chief artery linking north and south China, while also providing a means for the traditional rice tribute to reach Peking without the hazards of a sea voyage. In some places it was a hundred feet wide, its sides faced impressively with stone. In others it was merely a tortuous muddy channel winding monotonously through level country.

At strategic settlements where roads and feeder canals led into the interior we stopped and called on leading local merchants to persuade them to become our dealers. Or if we already had a dealer in the community, we helped organize his sales forces and went with him to visit stores where our products could be sold. Sometimes, surrounded by the street crowd which always formed when foreign devils were present, we lit sample cigarettes and after taking a few puffs ourselves, handed them to bystanders or thrust them into the toothless mouths of grinning old men who in eighty years had never puffed anything but pipes. All of this was accompanied by much good-humored banter and by-play, occasionally by resentful catcalls reminding us that we were interlopers. Meanwhile our trained crews would be roaming the streets, plastering the walls with advertising posters, distributing additional samples, and generally drumming up trade. It was all part of the white man's potent big medicine that was changing the face of Asia and the world supposedly for the better.

One night when we were moored to a levee whose top had loomed four feet above the deck when we went to bed, I felt a gentle lifting sensation while sleeping. Next morning we found ourselves nearly level with the levee's top and with the roofs of houses beyond. Soon the water was spilling over the levee, inundating miles of fertile land. It was the terrible Yangtze flood of 1910.

Cruising across country at housetop level we rescued as many survivors as we could carry, taking them to the nearest high ground, depositing them, going back for more. Sometimes we had to push dead bodies away with boathooks, sometimes resist the clutching hands of the living in order to save ourselves and our passengers from being swamped. Hundreds of thousands lost their lives. Millions were left homeless and starving. But in the long, often grim story of China it was merely an episode, one of time's little gestures.

Soon afterward I became the B.A.T. representative at Shih-Kiachwang, a strategic railroad and trading junction a hundred miles or so south of Peking. I traded on my own there, too, and also at Pao-ting-fu nearby, and then was posted to my final and favorite billet at Kalgan, on the Mongolian border, where the Great Wall dipped and rose across barren mountains, and the wild country beyond stretched unbroken for thousands of miles across Mongolia into Siberia and Turkestan, or to Sinkiang and Tibet. I'd come to the jumping-off place for the Far West of Asia—Asia having its Wild West then just as we in North America did, and its West being by that time remoter and wilder than ours.

At Kalgan the 150 miles of railroad from Peking ended in a dry watercourse. The town with its shops, stalls, earth-walled dwellings and compounds, sprawled along this watercourse for several miles. Its unpaved main street, which was also the caravan trail that led up through the huge gate in the Wall into Mongolia and all the hinterland, swarmed with strings of camels, ox carts, flocks of sheep, mule trains, horses, dogs, and people of many kinds. There were fierce-looking slant-eyed Outer Mongols dressed in their native sheepskins, somewhat smaller but equally slant-eyed Manchurians, turbanned Mohammedans from the Far West, the ever-present ever-industrious Chinese, Siberian Russians with fur caps, and we American, English, German and Scandinavian traders.

B.A.T. headquarters was situated in a compound built by Chinese railway engineers a short distance from the railroad station. Within its walls were godowns (warehouses), servants' quarters, stables, and our central bungalow with its galvanized iron roof, bedrooms, dining room, tack room, storeroom, and offices, surrounded by a wide verandah—and by enough space to assemble and load a camel caravan.

These were the last great years of the caravan trade, of methods and routes almost unchanged since the days of Marco Polo. Thousands upon thousands of camels departed and arrived in Kalgan annually. They carried tea, cigarettes, tobacco, candles, silks, cottons, and all the varied merchandise of the coastal lowlands to be exchanged for the wool, hides, and furs of the interior.

In and around our compound were men cut in a mold to do this work: the Norwegians Oscar Mamen and T.A. Rustad, embodying a Viking tradition turned landward rather than seaward from their Scandinavian homeland; W.B. Haughwout, a veteran American trader-adventurer; Frans August Larson, the Swedish missionary, trader, explorer, often called the Prester John of the twentieth century, and in fact an honorary Duke of Mongolia and one of the most effective yet modest persons I ever met. Larson later assembled the camels and guided Roy Chapman Andrews on the American Museum of Natural History's expedition into the Gobi that discovered the fossilized remains of dinosaurs and brought them back to New York. Without Larson's influence with the Mongol authorities at Urga, Andrews could not have accomplished what he did.

I was soon conducting camel caravans along the border and into the interior, meeting native leaders, dealing for livestock and merchandise, feeling in many respects as though I'd come full circle and was back to the life I'd known on the ranch. Even the countryside reminded me of Southern California with its vast deserts, barren mountains, and fertile grassland.

But now the violent forces I'd sensed underlying Chinese life broke out. The Chinese Revolution of 1911 had two basic purposes. One was to overthrow the tottering and corrupt rule of the Manchu Dynasty in Peking, the other to free China from foreign domination. Overriding both and often obscuring them was the terrible need of most Chinese simply to survive. Even in the best of times about ten percent of the population, pressed by hunger, was ready to rise, loot, rape, and murder at the least provocation. Millions more lived near the verge of starvation. Other millions had recently been rendered homeless and hungry by the floods.

Nevertheless it was, of all incongruous things, the proposed construction of a railroad in, of all unlikely places, the remote "tea province" of Szechwan that actually triggered the revolution. Szechwan lay isolated behind mountain ranges in the remote southwest corner of China bordering India, Burma, and Tibet. A controversial railroad was proposed there that would cut through the mountains and link Szechwan with the rest of the country. But the railroad would disrupt an age-old economy of carriers and carters and all their associated interests. Resistance to construction of the railroad became resistance to the Imperial Government in Peking—which had proposed it and proposed financing it by foreign loans. Imperialists and foreigners would be building the hated railroad.

This sparked riots in Szechwan in the spring of 1911. The spark spread elsewhere to students, young soldiers, and other reformers led primarily by Sun Yat-sen. Even in faraway Kalgan we heard rumblings of this. Our local commander declared himself irrevocably loyal to the Imperial Regime.

Fighting broke out at Wuchang on the Yangtze early in October 1911. It spread quickly to Hankow and Nanking. Both sides fought with extreme bravery. A number of foreigners participated in the field and behind the scenes. Most of them including Thomas and other British-American Tobacco leaders strongly supported Sun Yat-sen and the Republican cause. They believed that a republican government led by Sun, who'd been educated in the U.S., would be best for China and the Chinese and for foreign interests. Most of us in the field agreed.

My involvement came through a telegram from Thomas telling of trouble at Pao-ting-fu, the provincial capital ninety miles south of Peking where I'd done considerable trading, and asking if I could go at once to Peking for further information. Peking was said to be in turmoil. But I took the next train, got through without difficulty (learning later that they had recently removed piles of severed heads left in the streets after the fighting), and went directly to the B.A.T. office which was located on a side street just off the Chienmen or main thoroughfare.

There Jimmy Hutchison, our Peking manager, explained the situation at Pao-ting-fu.

Regional military leaders were seizing power as the central government at Peking weakened. Two warlord armies were jockeying for control of Pao-ting-fu. Fighting and pillaging were rampant. Our native dealer was holding a substantial quantity of silver which needed transportation to Peking. Numerous subdealers in outlying districts were in a similar predicament. Transporting the money under armed guard as was usually done was out of the question. Armed guards would be almost certain to attract the unfavorable attention of riotous mobs, bandits, or marauding soldiery. What was needed, according to Hutchison, was a small-scale, fast-moving operation which would collect the silver unobtrusively and bring it quietly to Peking. I had no illusions that the job would be an easy one but it could yield me a substantial bonus, enhance my standing with Thomas and B.A.T., and result in useful contacts I might exploit later.

I stayed overnight at Peking (our headquarters there included a dormitory and piano bar as well as offices and godowns), talked further with Hutchison and with Charlie Coltman, Standard Oil's district manager. Standard employed many of the same native agents in the Pao-ting-fu area as B.A.T., its chief stock-in-trade there as elsewhere being paraffin candles and coal oil. Standard had developed an inexpensive oil lamp, the *Mei-foo*, which provided light in millions of Chinese households and burned millions of gallons of U.S. kerosene. Like the rest of the Far East, China was becoming an important market for our mass-production and mass-marketing techniques.

A flatcar like this one with a mounted machine gun and a detachment of soldiers preceded our train during the trip from Peking to Pao-ting-fu.

Hutchison and Coltman furnished me lists of their agents in the Pao-ting-fu area plus letters of authorization and next morning I was on my way south by train accompanied by Lu, who by this time was a second-hand edition of myself in appearance. He wore my old clothes. They saved him money and made him fashionable since many Chinese were adopting western dress. Under his coat he carried a .38 Smith & Wesson in a shoulder holster as I did. In addition I carried my .303 British Winchester in hand.

Our train was preceded by a pilot locomotive pushing a flatcar manned by a squad of Imperial soldiers wearing caps and dark blue uniforms, commanded by a little Frenchman who symbolized the many foreigners who served the Peking government one way or another. Besides rifle and pistol his men were armed with a tripod-mounted, water-cooled machine gun. Peking was anxious to maintain control of the railroad, its only line running south to Hankow and the Yangtze region.

For reasons real or imaginary, our little Frenchman stopped his pilot locomotive frequently. Consequently we stopped too, never knowing quite what to expect. There were only a few passengers and most of them got off at wayside stations. As we poked along, I had time to survey the countryside which was flat as a pan and dry as dust, now in late autumn, with its stubble of wheat and barley and dry stalks of *kolyiang*—the tall millet—and to think about what to do when I reached my destination. Acquaintances there from earlier days might still be active and I thought of one in particular who might be able to help me—if she had escaped jail or beheading.

As we neared Pao-ting-fu, signs of trouble increased. Refugees jammed the roads. Some led loaded mules. Some pushed large wheelbarrows which had a wooden deck all around a central wheel, the deck stacked high with possessions. Others lined both sides of the tracks hoping for a ride anywhere out of the district.

By the time we reached the station at the outskirts of the city, the crowd had become enormous. I made my way through it to the depot building and sent a wire to Peking saying I'd arrived and the lines were still open. Then I told the first beggar I met to fetch me the Queen of the Beggars. Given such a crowd, I guessed she'd be nearby. Sure enough, in a few minutes here she came. She wore her usual ragged padded trousers and jacket. Her face was wrinkled as a sunburned mummy's. A few gray hairs were drawn to a bun at the back of her head and when she smiled I could hardly see a tooth. For a woman worth in all probability a good many thousands of dollars, she was well calculated to fool a man.

"Illustrious Master is welcome!" she began in her usual vein, twinkling and bowing like a sing-song girl.

"I thought I'd find you and your rascals somewhere in a crowd like this!" I rejoined.

When we'd exchanged pleasantries, I asked her if she would guard my silver there on the station platform while I collected it from outlying districts. I knew it would be as safe in the custody of the beggars and thieves, their accomplices, as in a bank.

Thieves and beggars were an integral part of Chinese life and absolutely dependable if you knew how to deal with them. At Kalgan, for instance, when we wanted a night watchman we sent for the head of the thieves' guild. "I have just the man for you!" he replied, when we told him our needs. The man he sent us was too old and decrepit to scale walls or break into freight cars and would have been a burden for the union to support unless they found him an easy job such as nightwatchman. We paid him twenty dollars a month, as much as we paid our cook, and he would amble around the yard, rattling his wooden rattle box until ten o'clock to show he was on duty, and then lie down on the verandah outside the front door and sleep sound till morning. Not a thief ever entered our compound. If we'd hired an honest man to guard us, we'd have been stolen blind.

The Queen looked a little incredulous when she heard my proposal. "You'd trust me?"

"Why not?"

I could see she was deeply flattered. She bowed low. "Your silver will be safe! My people will be your people!"

I was counting on help from her people. They might turn up anywhere and come in handy at short notice: professional blind men and women, some with eye sockets like hideously gaping wounds; hunchbacks; skin-disease sufferers; pickpockets; young girls who hired babies by the day to beg with; ragged young toughs, handy with knives; all with plenty of savvy. Harassment was their usual tactic. If you didn't pay up, they'd dog your footsteps and abuse you at the tops of their lungs, embarrassing you publicly until you did. Merchants and other businessmen paid them off regularly or found a yelling rabble at the front door discouraging customers. At the end of the day, they handed their receipts over to the Queen and she kept her share and the guild's and returned them a percentage. And they had better not cheat. Guild discipline was absolute. Unswerving honesty and obedience were its primary rules. Infraction usually meant death.

With the beggars and thieves on my side I felt I'd made a good beginning. Next I needed transportation into the old walled city which lay two miles away. Po-ting-fu was the capital of Chihli, a rich fertile province resembling portions of our American Middle West.

Produce from the interior reached it by canal boat and caravan trail, and was transshipped northward by rail to Peking or Tientsin. The city was notorious because the Boxer Rebellion had started there with the beheading of American missionaries and had spread over China, involving not only foreigners but their Chinese associates, such as my Lu, and especially Chinese Christians who were murdered by the hundred. We finally found a carter willing to sell us his services though he protested loudly that only persons of great courage such as himself were willing to reenter the threatened city.

I talked with the Queen of the Beggers, my ally during the troubles at Pao-ting-fu.

Inside the walls there was an atmosphere like that of a quiet autumn day before a winter storm. As the Queen had explained to me, this was due to the fact that in typical Chinese style, neither of the opposing warlord armies wanted to risk a battle by advancing into a city which they both coveted. While their commanders negotiated, troops looted the surrounding countryside. Hence the crowds of refugees.

A number of people had elected to remain in Pao-ting-fu, nevertheless. You have to frighten a Chinese badly to make him leave the place his family has occupied for centuries, and though some shops were closed and their shutters down or their boards up, others were open and there was a considerable amount of activity.

At the B.A.T. office, our representative, an unusually apprehensive type, was expecting me. His silver dollars were wrapped in paper in rolls of twenty and packaged in amounts of one thousand with burlap and rope. His bulk silver was in the form of shoes, literally little ingots of silver four to five inches long, cast, so tradition said, in the shape of some long-dead empress' slippered foot. I don't know how far back in time the shoes dated—probably not as far as the bronze knife money I found in one of the buried cities of Mongolia—but far enough. They ranged in value from five taels (about $5.50 Chinese or roughly $2.75 U.S.) to 100 taels, depending on the amount of silver each contained—a tael (approximately 1⅓ ounces) being worth a little less than 60 U.S. cents. There was no gold, China being a silver-standard country, and we didn't bother with paper bills, or cash (the money with the hole in the center) or other copper coins.

"The soldiers may enter the city at any moment," he warned me. "You must hurry if you are to return to Peking safely."

"I must visit your outlying dealers first," I reminded him, "and collect their money. Have you notified them?"

He assured me he had.

"I'll need transportation. I understand carts are impossible to procure. Are there mules?"

He looked as if I'd asked for flying carpets.

"There is no livestock left in the area. Marauding soldiers have seen to that!"

"Nevertheless I must have mules or horses and carts."

Seeing he couldn't get rid of me or his money until he had solved my problem, he remembered there might be mules at a village nearby.

Lu found us two rickshaws and we went to the village in record time. There I persuaded the owner of the mules that since his precious animals would likely be confiscated by the soldiers anyway, he might as well rent them to me at a spanking good price and get what he could out of them while he still owned them.

They were good mules. Each could carry 300 pounds. With him and two muleteers to help us, we headed for the remotest village on my list. Scraps of red cloth tied to our mules' manes proclaimed us to be under the protection of the beggars and thieves. Sometimes a gang of ragamuffins escorted us armed with knives and even a few guns. More often a solitary figure emerging from a crowd of refugees, and disappearing back into it, informed us which way was safe and which not.

Reaching the most distant village we proceeded along a deserted street until we came to a sign announcing in Chinese characters and English letters that this was the agency for the British-American Tobacco Company or "*Ying-Mei yen-ch'ao kung-ssu*" and also Standard Oil, "*Kong-lee hung-lung*," literally: "Universal profit and great prosperity company."

Inside a walled compound were huts for coolies and servants, stables, warehouses, the merchant's house, and his office—a small room where the old fellow was sitting behind a counter in a comfortable chair, his sons and grandsons hovering nearby in case he needed anything, while in the background clerks at tables pored over ledgers as if nothing unusual were happening anywhere in the world.

To exhibit anxiety in time of crisis was out of the question, here where they were most exposed. He led me through the little gate in his counter and invited me to sit down.

Tea was served. I asked after the health of his family, he asked about me and my affairs. Then I showed him my letters of authority and we got down to business. His accounts were in order, his money ready on the floor of the office packed in burlap. While his boys and Lu marked and numbered the bundles with lampblack, he showed me—never hurrying—through his warehouses. They were well stocked with our cigarettes—Honest Weight in zinc-lined wooden cases of 50,000 capacity that cost $68 each; Peacocks costing $225; Pirate, $190; and the fancy Three Castle brand in round tins of 50 which officials and the military smoked.

When all was ready I signed a receipt for a certain number of silver dollars and shoes belonging to B.A.T. or Standard Oil, as the case might be. Had there been time to count the money I wouldn't have bothered to. The honesty of such veteran merchants was beyond question. Early in its operations, B.A.T. set up a contingency fund for losses, but over the years it grew so large from being unused that they invested it in something else. Bowing, hands hidden in the loose openings of opposite sleeves, the old man wished us on our way.

After several such stops, our mules were loaded and we hurried back to Pao-ting-fu where the Beggar Queen was waiting at the depot. With help from her people, we unloaded our cargo onto the platform while the crowd watched hungrily. It must have guessed what our packages contained. But the Queen's reputation was fearsome. At the first sign of trouble a war whoop would go up from members of her gang scattered through the crowd and out would come their knives. No one knew but what the stranger next him was a beggar or thief with a long knife. My presence and my Winchester were an additional restraint. Probably weighing more heavily in our favor was the ingrained Chinese respect for authority, plus the dominant role of the foreigner in national affairs.

When we'd unloaded, I handed the old girl a carton of cigarettes. We left her seated on our bundles of silver, puffing away contentedly.

On our third swing through the countryside we encountered the Chinese Jews. The first was a tall straight-backed fellow who approached me while we were loading silver in an agent's compound. He was dressed native fashion with a pigtail hanging nearly to his heels but had unmistakable Jewish features. He stated politely that he came from a nearby village where they'd heard we were transporting money to Peking. Could we be so generous as to transport some for them at proper fee? Legend had it that these so-called native Jews were descended from one of the ten lost tribes of Israel. Originally there were of course twelve Jewish tribes but after the Babylonian Captivity only two remained in the land called Palestine. The others disappeared somewhere, no one knows where for sure, but some must have made their way deep into Asia, because Marco Polo and other travelers recorded meeting them in China centuries later. Those I knew were several inches taller than any Jews I'd seen before and were quite distinct from those of the commercial Jewish colonies of Shanghai and Tientsin which were of comparatively recent origin.

I asked the young man why he thought his silver would be safe in my hands. He said his people recalled me from the days when I had traded in their area for B.A.T., based on my headquarters at Shih-kia-chwang. I remembered his village. It was exceptionally prosperous and well kept, had a mixed population, Jews and Chinese, and all the Jews wore Chinese dress. They had their synagogue and the Chinese authorities permitted them freedom of worship. Most of the men were peddlars working the countryside with backpacks or ran shops in town, but some were farmers and tilled good crops.

I said I might handle his money if there wasn't too much of it and that it might end up in the Hong Kong-Shanghai Bank in Peking if we had luck, but I could make no promises and he would have to bring it to me quickly. I showed him how we were packaging it and he sent a runner back. In little more than an hour, his first wheelbarrow arrived, its deck piled high with bundles of silver, one man pulling, another pushing. We took a good many thousand from that Jewish community, mostly in silver shoes.

When we'd collected all the silver from the outlying districts and finally from our Pao-ting-fu dealer, there were a good many hundredweight of it on the station platform. It would customarily have been transported to Peking by railway passenger-car but I had no such car. Also I had more silver than customary. Time was another urgent factor. The military stalemate was breaking up, the Queen informed me. The Army of the West, pushing across from Hsinchow, was whipping the Army of the South, driving up from the Yangtze, and Pao-ting-fu was due for the kind of rape only half-starved Chinese troops can give a city. "Master has but a few hours to complete his work!" she warned.

There seemed only one solution. I commandeered a freight that was headed south toward Hankow, told the engineer to cut his locomotive loose and back it into the "Y" in the yard with one empty boxcar, and then pull up to our platform. When he hesitated I showed him and the train officials my papers and my rifle. Standard Oil and B.A.T. could, and did, settle later with the government transportation authorities. It was my job to get the silver to Peking.

The Queen's boys and girls helped load it aboard our car, leaving space in the middle for Lu and me to move from door to door, and I saw that Lu had performed one of his minor miracles. From somewhere he'd acquired a battered straw armchair. There it stood, between the piles of silver, for Master to sit in.

Before departing I gave the Queen a package containing five hundred silver dollars. Something like moisture appeared in her dry old eyes. She bowed low. "This is too much honor for one so unworthy!"

She'd been sitting on many times that amount and could have sold me out at any moment but like an honest thief had kept her word. The last I saw of her she was bowing and smiling, her gang clustering eagerly around her, the crowd staring in wonder and envy.

Pao-ting-fu was sacked and burned a few days later but I felt sure she had survived, being, in her very Chinese way, an expert in the art.

During the early stages of our train ride to Peking, we kept a sharp lookout, Lu at one door, I at the other. But when all went well mile after mile I sat down in that inviting armchair. Lulled by the motion of the train, I soon dozed off. I was awakened by an unpleasant sensation. We were slowing down. I heard a sharp cry of alarm from Lu. Grabbing my rifle, I jumped to the open door.

Standing waist-deep in a field of dry *kolyiang* stalks a few yards away, ten or fifteen soldiers were deployed as if to waylay us. The engine had separated itself from our car and was pulling off up the line while we coasted to a standstill. I slapped my rifle to my shoulder and put a couple of quick rounds into the cab. They evidently ricocheted around in there in convincing fashion because the engineer slowed to a stop. I motioned him to back up. He obeyed with such enthusiasm that the recoupling nearly knocked us off our feet, while the men in the field watched as if transfixed. I hoped they'd stay that way. To make sure, I was playing my rifle muzzle over them and acting like I knew exactly what I was doing. "Always act with authority," as Thomas had said. I yelled and motioned at the engineer to get going toward Peking. The soldiers continued to watch while we pulled away. I decided they were a foraging party expecting to find something to loot in our boxcar, but I didn't stop to ask.

When we were a mile or two safely up the line, I told Lu: "Don't ever get me another straw armchair! And now throw this one out of here as far as you can!" He did.

We reached the main Peking station outside the Chienmen Gate about four in the afternoon. I'd wired ahead. Carts, armed guards, and B.A.T. people met us and escorted us and our money straight to the Hong Kong-Shanghai Bank, then as later China's most prominent. We arrived after closing time but the crew was still on duty and as soon as the necessary receipts were signed, the clerks began counting our money. With deft movements of thumb and forefinger so quick your eye could hardly follow, they flipped the dollars into their proper bins: Suchow dollars here, Hong Kong dollars there. Almost every province had its dollar, each a little different in value. The national standard was the Mexican dollar worth forty-eight U.S. cents but some were worth only forty-four, some forty-six and so on.

It looked like a mess but the clerks got it sorted out and I saw that Standard Oil and B.A.T. funds and those from the Jewish community were kept separate, and then I went off to report to Hutchison at B.A.T. headquarters, enjoy a warm reception at our piano bar, and sleep around the clock.

So ended my first freelance job for Thomas and the Company. It established me willy-nilly as successful troubleshooter. Thereafter I was apt to get a telegram from time to time offering me similar opportunities, and these led me into further adventures.

In the sixteen-mile pass that lay between Kalgan, China, and the crest of the Mongolian Plateau, one of our caravans stops to rest. There were more than 500 camels in this caravan but only about a hundred are showing. I am on the white horse at the far right.

3.

Journey to Kumbum

BACK AT KALGAN in the lee of the Great Wall, I resumed the life of caravanner and trader and was soon conducting caravans to Urga, 900 miles northwest across the grassy Mongolian Plateau and Gobi Desert, or along the border northward to Manchuria, or southwesterly into west China and northern Tibet.

Hampering our movements at this time was the fighting between Mongols and Chinese which had broken out along the border. Taking advantage of the turmoil caused by the Chinese Revolution, the Mongols were staging a revolution of their own after several hundred years of subjugation to China. They wisely avoided direct confrontation with an enemy who greatly outnumbered them. Operating in small units they struck at the flanks and rear of the Chinese, annihilating isolated detachments, disrupting supply trains, withdrawing swiftly into the recesses of their plains and mountains after each attack.

The Mongol fighting men were all horsemen, all mounted on the tough ponies whose forebears had carried Jenghis Khan and his forces triumphantly across Asia and much of Europe, earning their masters the name of Tartars, or literally "horsemen from hell." Some Mongols still carried the curved swords of that earlier era in addition to rifle and pistol.

The Chinese were at a disadvantage as they inched forward into Mongolia from bases such as Kalgan, trying to mount a conventional military campaign against an adversary they seldom saw. As consequence, hostilities sputtered along, neither side bleeding much, while marauding deserters, bandits, and freebooters helped make the border unsafe for caravans like ours.

Complicating things further, we were dealing with both sides. Our caravans originating in China often reached destinations in Mongolia Some of them carried contraband of war, unofficially of course, as did one in particular which I took to Urga in the spring of 1913.

It was a comparatively small caravan of 200 camels. They were, needless to say, the two-humped long-haired Bactrian camels, not the one-humped dromedaries of Egypt and Arabia. Each carried 500 pounds of cargo if a female, 550 if a male. Their loads, slung in rope slings, included bales of silk and cotton cloth, candles, tea, whiskey, gin, tobacco and cigarettes, and interspersed among some of the four-foot-long- eighteen-inch-deep bulk-cigarette cases—such as those I described in the warehouse near Pao-ting-fu—were special cases containing cigarettes with steel barrels and wooden butts. Others contained ammunition. These special packages of "smokes" reached us through a British trading firm in Tientsin. The rifles were distinguished by the "Peacock" label. Ammunition traveled under the "Three Castles" brand.

Running such cargo through Chinese military lines was risky but profits were high. For protection we relied heavily on the British flag, which as I've suggested was respected and feared the world over. We always flew it from a staff stuck in the pack of the first and last animals in our trains. For further deterrent, there was our own firepower. But if stopped and searched we stood a good chance of losing not only our cargo but our heads.

We left Kalgan on May 1 at 6:30 A.M. and wound up the pass toward the Mongolian Plateau. I remember the date and time of our departure because for one of the few occasions in my life I was keeping a diary. The reason for keeping the diary was because my life insurance was only collectible if I demised in the line of duty (and not in some frivolous escapade), and if I didn't come back from this trip, perhaps my diary would and I wanted a certain person in San Francisco to be better off because of me. I'd met her during my last fling there. She was petite, fiery, indomitable, red-haired, and to me very beautiful if no longer young.

Wong, my number one camel puller, a husky young giant, led the way as usual. Behind him, attached nose to tail by a light tough cord or "string," followed ten heavily laden pack camels. Then came Ho-bar with his ten camels. And so on, until we looked like a long dark snake crawling up the rocky pass between the barren mountains. I roved here and there on Jenghis, my gray Mongol pony, to see that all went well. Other outriders, similarly mounted, served as scouts and security guards.

After reaching the plateau, we took the East Road toward Manchuria hoping to skirt the edge of the fighting and reach Urga, the

With two of my camel boys. Note the traditional snuff box hanging from the neck of the one at my left.

Wong was my number-one camel boy.

Mongol capital, by a circuitous route. We covered seventy *li* (a *li* is the equivalent of one third of a mile) that first day without trouble and after twelve hours arrived at Da-hung-yo, a border point.

On May 2 we again traveled by day for greater safety. Usually we traveled at night because camels will not graze after dark and consequently must be pastured during daylight hours. We covered the ninety *li* between Da-hung-yo and Hi-swee-ker without serious incident, stopping for lunch at 2:30 with Dalomma, a Mongol duke and military leader who was effectively harassing, or so he claimed, some 10,000 Chinese with his 600 horsemen. The main body of Chinese troops was several miles farther into Mongolia, so incoming stragglers told us.

We departed Hi-swee-ker at 5:00 P.M. in order to bypass Chinese posts after dark if possible. When traveling by night we adopted a close-order formation for better protection. All strings drew up abreast forming a phalanx, a few yards between each string, outriders in close, no talking, no smoking. It is astonishing how quietly such an ungainly looking animal as a camel can move. With its bell clappers muffled (as customary after dark when on the trail in hostile territory) a caravan can pass within a few feet of you and you wouldn't know it unless you heard the squeaking of the pack ropes.

On May 3 we reached Hao-to-ho without difficulty, meeting only small detachments of Chinese. They said they were ordered to guard the road against surprise attack by Mongols. At Hao-to-ho we rested a day as customary during early stages of a trip. It gave us a chance to tighten the ropes with which our packs were slung and tied. They were made of new Chinese hemp which always "gave" a little during the first days.

To unload his camels, a boy made his entire string kneel. Then he removed the wooden pin that held the slings together across the tops of the packsaddles and the loads slid gently onto the ground at either side. Leaving the saddles on, he undid the strings that tied his camels one to another, and turned them out to graze, guarded by dogs and mounted men.

Chained to the last camel of each string and always turned loose to guard them when they grazed was a large fierce Mongolian camel dog. Camel dogs were born, raised, and spent their entire lives with camels. They were the fiercest dogs I ever encountered, fiercer than the most ferocious Alaskan dogs. I've known Mongol camel dogs to kill a wolf, something few Alaska-Yukon dogs could do. I've also known them to kill some of the human marauders who invariably attempted to steal our camels or to peel off and steal their valuable hair. Watch as we might, these thieves were so clever that they slipped past dogs and watchmen and stripped hair off some of our camels even by daylight.

At Koku-tu-su on May 5 I shot our first antelope for camp meat. He was one of the large Roman-nosed variety, weighing probably 400 pounds. As customary I shot him while a Mongolian-Tibetan prayer wheel was stuck down the back of my shirt collar. The prayer wheel was made of wood and looked like a child's rattle. It consisted of a hollow top which revolved on the end of a handle. Inside the top were scraps of paper on which prayers were inscribed in Tibetan. In theory the top was supposed to be turning as the result of the motion of your hand or the wind, and the prayers thus activated at the moment of killing an animal whose flesh was to be eaten. This supposedly prevented evil spirits from entering the meat. For morale purpose I was obliged to carry a prayer wheel when killing game for camp use or my boys—and Mu-Yan—wouldn't eat it. There was usually enough breeze blowing to make the top revolve and if there wasn't, no matter, ritual had been observed.

We flew the British flag from the first and last camels of our caravans. Rope slings held our bulk cigarette cases in place.

Mu-Yan, my Mongolian camel girl, was no beauty but she could sling a pack with the best men of my caravan crew. She was an excellent shot with a rifle and performed well under fire during bandit attacks.

I should say a word further about Mu-Yan. She was a typical camel girl, or woman to be exact. A career girl, we'd say today, though her expectations were not aimed toward the typewriter or an executive suite. Her husband had been killed in a fight, her children were staying with her parents, and she was out making her living as a number of Mongol women did—caravanning. Generally speaking, Mongol women enjoyed great personal freedom. In domestic affairs they had equal rights with men. Divorce was simply a matter of mutual agreement. Property was divided proportionately to its ownership at the time of marriage. Before or after marriage, a woman was expected to take as many lovers as she wanted. In fact it was common courtesy for a husband to offer you his wife if you stopped at his tent for the night. Or she might offer herself to you. Either way the next move was yours, and the only acceptable excuse was to plead disease or religious vows. Mongol women conducted themselves as your equals. They rode horses and camels, riding astride like men, acted as herders—cowgirls—and conducted business transactions. Some even became lamas and performed religious rites. Our supposedly advanced western nations offered nothing like it. Thus Mu-Yan could sling a pack with the best of my boys and when we were attacked by bandits she would "dzuk" her string of camels down prone and take shelter behind her own mount and bang away at the enemy over his back with her old Russian army rifle.

At Koku-tu-su a gale was blowing. We were getting out toward the northern Gobi. One flying cobblestone broke a lens in my glasses. I wore motorcyclist's goggles to protect my face during these windstorms. Sometimes they lasted three or four days and blew so hard we had to lie flat under our tarpaulins, because no tent would stand up in them. Our camels lay down too and gradually became covered by sand and pebbles until they were almost invisible, while the shaggy-haired ponies turned their rumps to the wind and bowed their heads stoically.

These enforced layovers, as well as many nights around trail campfires, gave me a chance to talk intimately with my Mongols about many subjects. A favorite one was the big meteor which had passed over Mongolia a few years before and crashed into the Siberian forest to the north, leaving devastation for many miles. Every Mongol was convinced it had passed directly over his yurta, lighting up the countryside as bright as midday. By nature, the Mongols were as simple, generous, cheerful, and brave a people as I ever knew.

Another thing they were sure about was their historical greatness as a people. The tradition of Jenghis Khan was still strong and they believed his spirit would return and the Mongol people rise again to prominence as in the days when they ruled the largest empire the world has ever seen, in terms of population and real estate, extending from the China Sea to the gates of Vienna and from the Siberian steppe to India and Persia.

I learned of their mystical faith in the God of Earth which they worshiped every mid summer from the top of the nearest hill. They prostrated themselves on the ground and called upon the god to listen to their prayers for relief from drought, pestilence, all manner of ills. On these occasions, a variety of selected young animals—a calf, a kid, a lamb or foal—were dedicated to the god, tagged with special bits of colored cloth, turned back into their herds to be spoken of for the rest of their lives as the God of Earth's animals and never killed, sold, or used in any way until the god called them to him in death.

Beyond Koko-tu-su Chinese soldiers were blocking the East Road so we moved out across country. From Mongol riders we learned that scouting parties of Chinese cavalry were in the hills ahead. Reportedly they were seizing all caravans claiming "contraband of war." But we managed to avoid them.

On May 7 we covered only fifty *li*, first dodging Chinese troops and then stopped by rain. Rain can be disastrous to a camel train. Loaded camels can't keep their footing on moist ground. They slip and fall and frequently injure themselves seriously. We had to stop and stack goods and spread tarpaulins.

On May 8 we rested all day. I gave the crew a treat by buying a fat-tailed sheep from a nearby camp. Sheep was considered a great delicacy, particularly the fat tail. Sometimes the tails grew so large and heavy they dragged on the ground and became infected, so the Mongols built little wooden carts or "trailers" which could be attached as supports and kept them from dragging. We ate the greasy boiled meat with our fingers or mixed it with millet in our eating bowls—I foregoing my sahib-style tin plate with knife and fork for this occasion.

Five thousand Chinese soldiers were reported forty *li* to the east and four thousand to the west. Twenty-five hundred Mongols were said to be one to two days ahead. Sorting the truth out of such rumors and then choosing the best way to proceed kept us busy.

By now we were zigzagging to avoid trouble, sometimes traveling 100 *li* a day in order to advance sixty. I could not help but side with the Mongols in their efforts to gain freedom from Chinese rule. Since my crew were Mongols, it increased this sympathetic feeling and gave us good standing with the native population as we progressed deeper into Mongolia. From the air we would have looked like a naval convoy on a sea of grass; our heavily loaded camels the cargo ships, our outriders the surrounding cruisers and destroyers. At one stage we broke up into several small units, each with a leader who knew the country, the better to infiltrate the Chinese lines.

Finally after a roundabout trip of forty-five days we reached Urga and disposed of our cargo at a good profit.

I'd hoped for a period of rest and relaxation after what had been a more strenuous trip than usual, but such was not to be.

●●●

Urga, capital and holy city of the Mongols, lay in a broad bare valley in the lee of a steep, almost treeless mountain range, where the Mongolian grasslands ended and the Siberian forests began. Like a frontier American town, its streets were unpaved. Some of its buildings and compounds were made of unpeeled logs, some of milled lumber, some of brick and stone. Roundabout it not Indians but nomad Mongols pitched their circular felt tents or yurtas and pastured their herds of horses, sheep, and camels. The twentieth century had hardly touched Urga. Electricity, plumbing, telephones were unknown. Its streets were littered with offal and refuse, rotting carcasses of animals, even the heads and limbs of humans dragged in from burial grounds by ravenous dogs, or attacked and killed while walking at night.

The town was divided into Chinese, Mongol, and Lama districts, the Chinese being the merchants and traders as usual, and the Lama district being the center for a population of many thousands of red-robed priests who lived in its huge lamasery, officiated in its temples, or served in the official residence or palace of the Living God, their Grand Lama and revolutionary Emperor. In addition there was a scattering of white foreigners, especially Russians, most of them traders like ourselves.

A few mornings after my arrival, Oscar Mamen, our Urga representative, and I were asleep in the house adjoining our compound when a young lama from the Imperial Palace walked into our bedroom shortly after daybreak and invited us to come to a conference. The impromptu nature of the invitation and the earliness of the hour were both in accordance with native custom, and we assumed the conference had something to do with our trading operations, the border war, or both.

As we approached the palace compound, the watchmen swung the heavy wooden gates in its high yellow wall. We rode our ponies into an earthen courtyard, tied them to posts near the main entrance, left our riding whips at the right-hand side of the door as custom dictated, and entered a long low antechamber floored with tile and lit by large candles. One of the lay brothers who officiated there (lamaseries usually had lay brothers and sometimes lay sisters—women beyond childbearing age—who with junior lamas performed menial tasks) received us and led us through corridors dim with age, smelling of dust, incense, and unwashed bodies, until we came to the room occupied by the Living God-Emperor and his advisors.

They were sitting crosslegged on the red-tiled floor on prayer rugs arranged in a semicircle. Overhead was a beamed ceiling, red lacquer between the beams, and here and there around the room low tables of Chinese blackwood and two or three braziers containing live coals to provide heat or to warm tea. "Sain-bai-na! (God be with you!)" they greeted us cordially, bowing over clasped hands. We returned the greeting, assuring them that we came in peace, and then sat down on rugs like theirs, crossing our legs in the standard manner.

Since we supplied them with many necessities of life besides munitions, we were on good terms with them. They operated an enormous business enterprise in connection with their lamasery, owning thousands of sheep, cattle, and horses, selling large quantities of hides and wool, much like the mission fathers of early California days. We bought their raw material and sold them tea, cloth, candles, cigarettes, and whiskey. Personally they were an extraordinary combination of sagacity and naivete. They were like red-robed Rip Van Winkles waking up into a modern world after centuries of sleep.

Their bare heads were shaved or closely cropped. The God's robe was a richer red, his sash a cleaner yellow than the others, and for this particular council of state—which seemed to be what it was—he had put on his ceremonial headdress, a crown perhaps twenty inches high, inlaid with gold, silver, and precious stones. Though he was the third greatest personage in the Lamaist world, ranking immediately behind the Dalai Lama of Lhasa and the Tashi Lama of Tashilhunpo, the Hutukhtu of Urga was largely the tool of his advisors, the hierarchy of senior lamas who actually exercised power. They indulged his childlike fancies, kept him pleasantly befuddled with liquor and women, and had organized the revolution against China using him as a figurehead. Though only in middle age, he was going blind from syphillis, syphillis being a national scourge because of the Mongols' extreme promiscuity and because so many lamas exercised their privileged status by taking any woman they fancied. The simple-minded Hutukhtu loved practical jokes and all kinds of mechanical gadgetry. When the Model "T" Ford sedan he had ordered as a curiosity reached Urga after being driven overland from Kalgan by a friend of ours, Ethan Le Munyon, who traded for the China-American Company out of Tientsin, curious Mongols, who had never seen an automobile before, nearly pawed the car to death before it ever reached the palace. To keep their hands off it Le Munyon wired its magneto to its body so that anyone touching it got a mild shock. This amused the God greatly. He invited a group of councillors of state to inspect his new toy, encouraged them to touch it, and was delighted when they snatched their hands away in consternation at the car's sting.

The God was a bit nutty about clocks of every description. He had a room full of them ranging in size from alarm clocks to grandfather clocks, all keeping time but no particular time, so that the din of their chiming, alarming, and cuckooing at odd intervals was truly remarkable. Many of them had been given him by foreign diplomats as presents, and Mamen and I had brought him several including a cuckoo clock purchased in Tientsin. He used to stand in front of it till the bird popped out and then clap his hands in delight.

Despite his childishness, he was a good man at heart and sincerely devoted to the cause of Mongolian independence.

He began by apologizing for disturbing our slumbers but explained that there was important business at hand that needed our sagacious attention. In addressing us he used our native names, "Horse Gate," (a literal translation of "Mamen" into Mongolian) and "Sh-lo-ta" which was as close as Mongols or Chinese ever came to pronouncing "Schroder."

The Minister of War, a senior lama who often pedaled over to our compound on his Russian bicycle, continued the conversation. "Unless the military situation along the border improves, our revolution may fail. This would not help your trading enterprises."

We agreed that it would not, and he continued: "So far the princes (the semi-independent nomad rulers whose word was virtually law in their districts) have not rallied wholeheartedly to the support of the revolution. We have about 20,000 irregulars facing nearly 200,000 Chinese. We cannot hold our own indefinitely against such odds. There is one word, however, which will unite all Mongolia and send it against China like the blow of a single sword."

"And what is that word?"

"The word of his Most Sacred Holiness, the Tashi Lama."

The Mongols were, as I've suggested, devout adherents of the Lamaism which stemmed from Tibet and particularly from its two great lamas, of which the Dalai was the more powerful politically but

The Hutukhtu of Urga. (F.A. Larson)

The Hutukhtu's bodyguards.

the Tashi (or Panchen) more powerful spiritually, especially in Mongolia. Later we learned that they had already secured the support of the Dalai Lama and in addition wanted the backing of the more popular Tashi or "Red God."

"And how will the word of the Red God help?"

"It will legitimize the revolution. When the highest god speaks, even a prince will listen. It will protect your trading privileges, Sh-lo-ta and Horse Gate. It will unite our people. United we cannot fail to defeat the Chinese though they be numberless as the blades of grass!"

"How does one secure the word of the Tashi Lama?"

"We are planning to send an emissary to Kumbum. Will you accompany him?"

We were taken aback to say the least. Kumbum Lamasery was about a thousand miles away and neither of us had been there or had any previous contact with the Tashi Lama.

We said we felt honored to be considered worthy of their confidence. "Who would accompany us to Kumbum?"

"Our colleague, your friend, the Hutukhtu of Lama Miao."

It was a good choice. The Hutukhtu or High Lama of Lama Miao was the administrative head of Lamaism in Mongolia. He lived at a comparatively small but important monastery on the border not far from Kalgan and was thus a southern or Inner Mongol, whereas the clique in Urga were northern or Outer Mongols. His support might give unity to an appeal to the Red God. But why they chose to involve us in the matter we were never quite sure. Partly it may have been because we did so much business with them, partly because they knew we were risking a good deal—a good deal more than our Russian counterparts who supplied them quite easily from nearby Siberia—by running guns through the Chinese lines and had thus demonstrated our loyalty; and partly it may have been due to our connection with the foreign power structure in China and the Far East, which they supposed to be greater than it actually was. In any event, foreign advisors were in fashion. Larson, our fellow trader, would soon be serving both them and the Chinese government in such a capacity.

After thinking it over we decided to do it. Besides strengthening our relationships in Urga, it would take us into new trade territory and give us a chance to make contacts we might exploit later.

According to their plan we were to go to Lama Miao, join our friend the Hutukhtu there, proceed with him and his retinue to Kumbum in the high country of northern Tibet.

We decided Mamen had better stay in Urga to look after our affairs while I, who was well acquainted with the border region and with the Bogdo of Lama Miao, made the trip.

I left before noon that day with a half dozen of our best Mongol horsemen.

We traveled at the traditional cross-country pace: lope five or six miles, slow to a jog or walk, then lope again. The distances you could cover in a day's riding in such manner over the rolling Mongolian grassland exceeded anything I had experienced, but even they were exceeded by the professional dispatch riders, forerunners of our pony express, who were still crisscrossing the country on regular routes as in the time of the great khans. Often these dispatch riders wrapped themsleves in cotton bandage cloth to support their limbs and reduce jarring and muscular strain. The cloth was applied over the clothing of the entire body, leaving only face and hands bare, as they raced across vast distances from station to station on relays of fast horses. We had no such wrapping and, in addition to weapons, carried dried meat and millet in our sausage-shaped canvas riding bags slung across the fronts of our saddles, but we changed horses often at herds that we passed and covered the 850 miles to Lama Miao in twelve days.

Lama Miao, reputedly the site of Kublai Khan's hunting lodge, stands at the edge of the Mongolian Plateau, where it breaks sharply away to the lowlands and the Imperial Forest that lie toward Peking. Wild apricots and rhubarb grow there in profusion. The hunting lodge or summer palace of Kublai Khan which reportedly stood nearby is described by Marco Polo as being of fantastic grandeur and dimensions. It was surrounded by a hunting park of vast extent including many varieties of animals and birds. Here the great Kublai spent the hot summer months of June, July, and August in the high cool air of Mongolia, his native land. And here he kept a stud of ten thousand horses and mares all white as snow, the story goes, and here Tibetan sorcerers performed such magic feats for their imperial master as causing full goblets of wine to rise from the sideboard and float through the air to his hand as he sat at table, and the weather to remain clear and sunny while storms raged roundabout.

Lama Miao, also called Dolon-Nor, was a major trade center where, as at Kalgan, the Mongols exchanged their sheep, horses, camels, hides, and wool for tea, tobacco, cotton, and silk of the Chinese. At the outskirts of the Chinese settlement was the Mongol community with its temples and a lamasery of some 2,000 persons.

The Bogdo or Holy One—old, shrewd, wise, and one of the best informed and most articulate lamas I ever knew—greeted me warmly. We were on familiar terms, he being among the good customers of our tea and candles, piece goods, cigarettes and whiskey. He seemed aware something was up, and when I told him the purpose of my visit and he had read the instructions sent him from Urga, he clapped his hands to command attention and began giving orders to his subordinates. Next day we were riding westward toward Kumbum, following the border road, Bogdo on a beautiful white pacing stallion and his attendant junior lamas mounted on geldings like the rest of us. Bogdo wore a Mongol hat of sheepskin partially peaked, with earflaps. His red robe was much faded. A dirt colored sash whose fringe showed that it had once been yellow surrounded his waist. A tobacco pouch made of skin hung from his sash; also his chopsticks-and-knife sheath. Inside the front fold of his robe he carried his silver eating bowl. Once that bowl had been wooden. Now that he was a head lama it was of silver. But he would still wipe it out with his finger after eating and lick the finger.

We numbered fifteen or twenty all together. Such parties were not uncommon in a land where everyone traveled horseback and my presence need arouse no suspicion since my trading operations along the border and business dealings with the lamas were well known. Nevertheless we avoided Chinese soldiers wherever possible.

We went at a brisk pace, the weather beautiful, the larks singing. They rose in circles, singing as they went, until lost from sight, when only their song came falling back to us like a melody out of the sky. Vast herds of antelope and gazelle scampered off to either side as we rode along. To occupy the time I engaged the Bogdo in one of our favorite topics of conversation: antiquities. Antiquities had interested me since boyhood days among the Spanish adobes and missions of California and my interest had been whetted by the many relics and ruins visible in China and Mongolia. Bogdo was well informed on those of the border region.

"This trip may take us near the pyramids of Shensi," he told me, the actual term he used being something like "man-made mountains."

"You mean burial mounds?" Burial mounds were common throughout China, many of them eight or ten feet high.

"These may be burial mounds but they are much larger than any you're familiar with. I have not seen them but they are said to be truly mountain-sized."

"Who built them?"

"No one knows. Our oldest books describe them as old many centuries ago."

"If they are so old and well known, why haven't I heard about them?"

"You foreigners make me laugh," he chided. "Because you haven't heard of something, you think it doesn't exist."

I made him promise to show me the pyramids if the opportunity presented itself when we reached Shensi province, and we continued westward along the border, bypassing Kalgan and following the high grassland toward Kuei-hua-cheng, another border town, where there was also a B.A.T. compound. As we approached it we passed near the missionary settlement of the Belgian Catholic Fathers, a kind of natural wonder in itself, which I described to the Bogdo.

Following the Boxer Rebellion, the Belgian Fathers had taken their indemnity—offered by the Chinese government for losses suffered—in the form of this fertile border land. "Father Rubbens' Valley" it was called after the founder of the extraordinary community there. It was a cross between a communal utopia and a poor farm. Needy Chinese families flocked to it from many parts of the country. Each family was given an allotment of land—ten *mou* or fifteen *mou* (a *mou* is one third of an acre)—depending on its need. The community helped them build their houses and loaned them seed, a pair of oxen, a plow, and food to sustain them until their first crop was harvested. They retained half that harvest. The other half went to the communal granary. Of that half, one half was sold to help pay expenses of the settlement, for such things as roads, mills, water wells, a hospital, police. The other half stayed in the granary as insurance against time of need.

Within three or four years the new arrivals were usually thriving. The Belgian Fathers thus won wide respect. Unlike other missionary groups they were entirely self-sustaining. They had their own flour mills, blacksmith shops, vineyards (the vines grown from cuttings supposedly taken from the Pope's own vineyards near Rome), and tobacco fields. They made their own clothes and even meerschaum pipes, one of which I smoked in addition to my Pierson. To protect their health they followed a regular program. Every afternoon about two o'clock they went to their houses, stripped down to their underwear, drank three eight-ounce cups of mulled red wine mixed with hot tea. After the first cup they were bathed in sweat. These regular sweats seemed to protect them from disease, especially the dreaded, louse-borne typhus which was very prevalent.

I enjoyed many a good sweat treatment with the Fathers, stopping by when on trips and leaving them English and American newspapers and magazines, sometimes coursing wolves with them after the pair of greyhounds which I gave them. They were not Belgian only, but French, Irish, and other nationalities as well and had their choice of serving in the Belgian Congo, the Philippines or the Mongolian border. They were hardy fellows, brooking no nonsense. When attacked by bandits they soundly defeated their attackers, the whole community rallying behind them using knives, pitchforks and old gas-pipe muskets. Tucking up their robes like battling bishops of medieval times, they and their "troops," led by the redoubtable Father Rubbens, pursued the fleeing attackers so fiercely that a number of the bandits ran right out of their shoes, which the thrifty priests collected and distributed to their needy people.

Perhaps the most interesting feature of their settlement was its girls' school. In most Chinese families a girl child was simply another mouth to feed. Baby girls were often strangled at birth, abandoned on rubbish heaps, or sold into slavery as household servants, concubines, or sing-song girls. Not so in Rubbens' Valley. They went to a school run by nuns and were taught to cook, sew, and keep house so that they might find good husbands. They were not allowed to marry until the age of sixteen. Then they were permitted the almost un-heard-of privilege of meeting and even refusing the offers of their suitors. If approved, a suitor was allowed to "buy" his girl by presenting her with a dowry which consisted of 150 tael, or about $105 in U.S. money. Of the 150 tael, ten went to her in cash, the balance taking the form of household utensils, clothing, and personal belongings. It was a considerable endowment. But there was more. At any time during the first year of marriage she had the right, clearly stated in her marriage contract, to complain to Father Rubbens in the event of mistreatment. There were few such complaints, however, and the demand for "Rubbens girls" as wives continued keen.

There was little evidence of organized religion in the settlement. Freedom of worship was the rule. Services were held but there was no compulsion to attend. Such freedom of choice was a further reason for the success of the colony, which was probably the most successful missionary enterprise anywhere in China or Mongolia.

Bogdo was impressed by my account. He said that such Christianity resembled Lamaism in that it mingled priests and people at workaday level sharing all aspects of life. Many lamas, it was true, lived away from the protection of lamaseries and were members of nomadic camps, or even lived alone, maintaining their own tents, flocks, and herds and, in the role of businessman, doctor, or priest, shared and made substantial contributions to the popular welfare.

At Kuei-hua-cheng we rested our animals, Bogdo and his lamas staying at the local temple while my boys and I went to the B.A.T. compound. The compound was a huge one, large enough to play polo in, and there was always plenty of livestock available, Kuei-hua-cheng being one of the main centers of the border and trans-Mongolian caravan trade. Finding all white men absent, I made arrangements with our capable Chinese manager, Lu, for a mule train to accompany us into the wild country ahead where we would carry our own food and water. Even had there been white men present, I would have dealt with Lu who handled all such practical matters, and without whom the foreign devils would have been quite helpless.

With a dozen big ungelded mules, probably tougher than any that ever came out of Missouri, packing 350 pounds apiece, and with an old gray bell mare to lead them, we went on west toward the Yellow River. The chief reason for the toughness of the domestic animals of Mongolia and the border region was the fact that they were never sheltered, shod, or fed. They fended for themselves, winter or summer, learned to survive wolves, blizzards, Gobi sandstorms, long cross-country trips that would leave an ordinary horse or mule a wreck. They were like the animals (and the men) of our early West and that was one reason for my affinity for them. Another reason was the gear they wore. Our mules, for instance, wore packsaddles almost identical with the *aparejos* I'd used on the ranch: leather pads stuffed with grass and stiffened with willow twigs, common in Mexico, too, and throughout the Southwest, dating back through the conquistadors to the Old World and time immemorial.

The river at Pao-ling Miao was lower than I'd ever seen it. It appeared impossible to cross with animals because of quicksand, so we turned south and followed the bank thirty or forty miles until we came to a ferry where there was a spectacularly large waterwheel, at least fifty feet high by twenty wide, lifting water to irrigate nearby fields, the water being caught and hoisted in five-gallon Standard Oil tins instead of the traditional wood buckets.

We were now entering Shensi, a province largely unknown to the outside world.

My friends R.S. Clark and Arthur Sowerby had explored parts of it four years before. Clark, a wealthy New Yorker, attached to our legation at Peking as intelligence officer, and Sowerby, the son of missionaries and field collector for the British and Smithsonian Museums, had penetrated Shensi down-river from the spot where we were entering, then turned south through Yenan-fu—a city which gained notoriety during the Second World War as headquarters of Mao-tse Tung and the Chinese Communists—and proceeded to Sian-fu [new spelling, Xian] and westward along the old Imperial Highway to Lanchow. Their purpose was to map unexplored territory and collect plant and animal specimens. We would take much the same route.

Crossing the river, we entered the Ordos Desert, a wasteland of shifting sands whose dunes may be the highest in the world. I know they are much higher than those of the Gobi to the north. Some rise fifty or sixty feet. They are the residue of winds that have blown across the Mongolian Plateau for ages, depositing sand

and dust always more and more to the southwest. The heavier sand settles out first.The dust or loess carries farther and finally lies to a depth of two hundred feet or more.

There is no possibility of riding against the Ordos dunes. You must travel with them as with a wind at sea, veering slightly this way or that if you wish, but never breasting them directly. Even when there is no wind their sand is constantly moving and gives off a continuous hissing sound. This is caused by the dunes breaking at their crests as high waves break and crumble. It goes on day and night much as the sea continues to move even in calm weather. Travelers, especially lone ones, are said to have been driven mad by it. It was eerie.

Our water skins, dried meat, and millet sustained us now as we made several dry camps and saw no game.

Continuing southwesterly we came to the Great Wall, completely covered by sand in some sections, only its watchtowers showing; and then we emerged into the region of the loess. Plateaus of pure dust, several hundred feet thick, were cut by sudden watercourses as sheer as crevasses in ice, and you had to be careful not to ride into them by accident.

Here I shot the giant bustard that has three toes and flies with the wild geese flocks. His flesh is as delicious as a turkey's, all dark except along the breast bone where it is white.

We began to see settlements again, some of them wholly or partially in ruins, grim evidence of the Mohammedan Rebellion of several decades earlier, the terrible civil and religious war which devastated western China and cost millions of lives, though the outside world heard little about it because the region was so remote. The Moslems rose periodically against their Chinese overlords, raised the ancient warcry of: "Death to unbelievers!" and were finally put to the sword themselves by the much more numerous Chinese. After which peace and toleration would reign for a while.

From time to time I reminded Bogdo of his promise to show me the wonderful man-made mountains he'd mentioned. He made inquiries at the monasteries where we sometimes stopped but no one seemed to have heard of them.

When there was no lamasery or inn available he could be quite arrogant about accommodations, sometimes ejecting families from their huts or tents so that his holiness could be housed. Generally he behaved himself well and collected information or propagandized for the Mongol revolutionary cause as we traveled, often engaging in long conferences with his red-robed brethren at our wayside stops. When I asked him how the Red God was likely to receive our request for assistance, he shrugged and replied enigmatically: "He already knows what we are going to say and what he will reply." This was in keeping with the widespread belief in the omniscience of the Tashi and Dalai Lamas. I remained skeptical.

Descending onto the plain of the Huei, a tributary of the Yellow River, we began to see many burial mounds. This was a region of very ancient settlement and its mounds were more numerous and elaborate than any I had observed previously, some rising to twenty or thirty feet. Again we made inquiries about man-made mountains but without success.

Farther along on the fertile plain at Sian-fu, the ancient capital of China, we had better luck. Sian is situated on the Imperial Highway or Old Silk Road, the main overland trade route between China and Europe in ancient times. Its population was around half a million and it was comparable to Peking in the impressiveness of its walls and some of its buildings. In the downtown section, watchtowers arched over the streets. The plazas in front of the *yamens*, or official headquarters, were crowded with buyers and sellers. Merchants advertised their wares by yelling at the tops of their lungs from booths roofed with straw matting or blue cloth. There were oranges and peaches for sale in the stalls; the profusion of fruits in China—pears, plums, apricots, grapes, persimmons—was always impressive to me. I wanted to see the stone tablet which supposedly told of the establishment of Christianity in Sian by missionaries from Palestine around 600 A.D. It had stood on a public street but had been removed to a place of safekeeping and I could not find it. The tablet was later copied, I learned, and a replica taken to the Vatican.

Inquiring of priests at the Lama Temple (Lamaism was prevalent in western China as in Mongolia) Bogdo discovered that our man-made mountains or pyramids might be found a day or two's travel westward.

From Sian, we followed the old caravan road that in Marco Polo's time carried the silks and spices of Cathay to the seaports of the eastern Mediterranean. It was a combination of cart track and nearby caravan trail, the trail—like most caravan routes—pounded hard as concrete by millions of feet over hundreds if not thousands of

This large flat-topped pyramid is located near Sian in western China. It may be a royal tomb. Expert analysis reveals its base width to be approximately 1,200 feet and its height approximately 500 feet.

years, and the cart track deeply cut—sometimes as much as six or eight feet—into the surrounding earth. Where it was paved with stone, wheels had worn ruts so deep that the axles of carts sometimes dragged. We held to the caravan trail and, sure enough, two days west of Sian we heard that the man-made mountains were said to be a day's travel farther north.

After a night at a village inn we headed northward at sunrise. It was farming country, not particularly isolated, villages here and there. Toward noon we saw something rising ahead that looked like a small mountain but its top was flat and it had regularly sloping sides. Before long we could distinguish the outlines of a huge pyramid. Then others began to appear. I'd heard of flat-topped pyramids in Mexico and South America and had seen photographs of the pyramids of Egypt, some of them flat-topped too, but never anything like this.

As we approached the big one we could see that trees and shrubs grew part way up its sides and that the sides had eroded into gullies and ravines. There were cultivated fields around it and a small village nearby. Stopping at the village we made inquiries. No one could tell us anything about the origins of the pyramids. They had "always been there." They were held in great veneration but no relics were known to have come from them. Yes, perhaps they were tombs, but who could say?

Upon close inspection I estimated the big one to be approximately 600 feet high and 1,500 feet wide at the base. It was truly a colossal structure, breathtaking and awe-inspiring. Its sides had been wholly or partly encased by a layer of rock but much of the rock had fallen or was covered by debris from above. The rock appeared to be cut field stone about three feet square. The core of the pyramid seemed to have been made of the pounded earth still commonly used for construction in China. Alternate layers of lime and clay are mixed and pounded. When the lime permeates the clay and hardens, the result is something like concrete.

Here and there at a distance of about 200 yards, the pyramid was surrounded by a low mound of earth, perhaps the remains of a wall that once enclosed a sacred precinct. But there were no signs of altars and temples or of doors or other openings into the pyramid itself.

I've since learned that these long known but little publicized pyramids or burial mounds are probably imperial tombs and may date to the third century B.C., perhaps earlier. Early European travelers reported them in various ways and a few years before us Arthur Sowerby and R.S. Clark saw some of them. A few years later an eccentric Britisher named Moore-Bennett measured a large one in the vicinity of Sian. It was probably not the big one I saw, for its height was only about 80 feet but its base width was quite similar, each of its four sides measuring between 1,200 and 1,400 feet, and it also was made of compressed earth and rock debris.

In 1947 my eye was caught by a photograph in a San Francisco newspaper. It was an aerial shot of a huge flat-topped pyramid resembling the one I saw. Its height was given as 1,000 feet and its base as about 1,500 feet square. It was described as situated in an isolated mountainous region near Sian. Its discoverer, if that is the proper word, was Colonel Maurice Sheahan, Far Eastern Director for Trans World Airlines which then operated in China under arrangement with the Chiang Kai-shek or Nationalist Government which had helped us win the war against Japan but was about to be taken over by the Communists.

Sheahan said the pyramid appeared to dwarf those of Egypt and was situated at the foot of the Tsinling Mountains some forty miles south of Sian and that a second flat-topped pyramid nearby appeared much smaller. He was quoted as saying he had flown over the large pyramid often during the war years on supply flights from Burma to China with the U.S. Air Force and been impressed by its perfect pyramidal shape. "I did not give it much thought during those years partly because it seemed incredible that anything so large could be unknown to the world," Sheahan said.

Dr. Phyllis Ackerman of the School for Asiatic Studies, New York, suggested that the story behind the pyramids "goes back 7,000 or 8,000 or more likely some 14,000 years" to the primitive cult of North Star worship. Estimating the big pyramid observed by Sheahan to be about 2,500 years old, Ackerman described it as possibly a religious site, possibly an emperor's tomb. She said that human sacrifices probably took place on its summit or within its sacred precinct, according to the account I read in *Science Digest*.

Ackerman may have been right in that star worship (focused on the North Star, the fixed point in the heavens, the constellation of the Great Bear, and the cardinal compass points) was evidently practiced by the early Chinese as by early peoples elsewhere, and I noticed that the pyramid was oriented with the compass points so far as I could tell.

At some early period in the history of China, colors were assigned to the four directions. Black was for the north, blue-green for the east, red for the south, white for the west. In the center was yellow. This may explain why the tops of the Shensi pyramids were flat and not pointed like most of those in Egypt. The flat tops were perhaps spread with yellow earth representing heaven.

We rode on for a look at the next pyramid, about three quarters of a mile away. It resembled the first but was only about two thirds as large. Nearby was a third one, still smaller and then a gap of several miles and then a southern group of four, all smaller still. All of the pyramids were flat topped, all had apparently been constructed by the same method, all were oriented to the cardinal compass points. Together they formed an irregular pattern with its apex at the big northern one.

Some believe that in the ancient world of mystery and magic the pyramid was a power symbol representing not only a sacred mountain but the cone or spiral which is an essential element in the natural order of things. Others believe that even today the pyramidal shape in any size represents occult power of various kinds, and that a miniature pyramid placed under your bed or office desk will enhance your sexuality or business success. I leave such speculations to the experts.

When I expressed myself duly impressed by what we had seen, admitting it was as remarkable if not more remarkable than anything I had beheld in the world of foreign devils, Bogdo was gratified. We agreed to ask the Tashi Lama about the pyramids, believing that if anyone knew their origins he would.

Old Bogdo began to weary during the later stages of our trip and at Lanchow-fu, a large commercial city where the Silk Road crossed the Yellow River, a city which later became the center for China's nuclear weapons production, I secured a traveling chair for him. It was a grand lama's chair, upholstered in royal blue, curtains at the windows. With a mule between the shafts at either end of it, Bogdo ascended into the Tibetan high country in style. Now and then he would poke his head out a window and shout or clap hands for something he needed. Often it was the wine skin which one of his young lamas hastened to bring him.

Tibet was regarded as beginning about 50 miles west of Lanchow and the old maps will show it that way. From there, Chinese authority diminished to near zero when you left the Silk Road—as we did about halfway in the 154-mile stretch between Lanchow and Liang-chow-fu—and headed southwestward into the hills.

As we entered Tibet the country became steeper and more barren but there were fertile valleys with good crops of beans and barley and prosperous villages. The blue-clothed Chinese disappeared and we began to see nomads dressed in sheepskins astride camels or tough shaggy ponies, or sometimes herding or riding yaks. Some of them stuck out their tongues at us in the usual Tibetan fashion as they smiled in greeting.

My colleague Oscar Mamen and some of the bales of licorice we brought back by caravan from the far west of China. Mamen, a noted adventurer, led Mongol guerrillas against Japanese invaders of Mongolia during World War II.

Mamen and I and Rustad went back into that country with a commercial caravan and sales crews several years later, distributing cigarettes and contacting local merchants at Lanchow and Liang-chow-fu along the way. Far to the west on the borders of Sinkiang, China's westernmost province right at the heart of Asia, we found an abundance of wild licorice which proved extremely valuable when the regular supplies from Persia and Turkey were cut off from Europe and the U.S. during World War I. We packed out thousands of tons of it and shipped them to the States. We also collected a number of valuable skins, including those of the white-faced bear and snow leopard. They used female urine to tan skins in that high country as was the practice among the Yukon Indians, female urine of course having a different chemical composition from male. A regular feature of hunters' huts was a small pot of it in one corner.

Kumbum Monastery was situated at the foot and up the sides of a barren mountain. It consisted of a scattered collection of buildings, most of them the one-storied flat-roofed whitewashed dwellings of lamas, here and there larger administrative buildings and impressive temples, some constructed in Tibetan style, some in Chinese. At its outskirts was a village and commercial center with shops and inns catering to the thousands of pilgrims who visited the monastery annually. Kumbum had been founded in the sixteenth century in honor of a reformer named Tsong Khapa who is supposed to have purified Lamaism of corruption and returned it to honesty. He was born near the monastery site and the locality had become a famous shrine attracting the faithful from Mongolia, Tibet, China, and even Siberia.

A welcoming party of young lamas (news of our coming had preceded us) met us at the gate and conducted Bogdo and his attendants in one direction, my boys and me in another.

En route to the guesthouse we passed one of the main temples. Pilgrims were prostrating themselves before it. Some were working their way up its steps and inside, a prostration at a time. It was not uncommon for them to travel halfway across Asia, prostrating themselves at every step. Inside, as I learned, were numerous images in gilt and bronze. In front of each was a metal basin or dish where you could leave your offerings in the form of food, money, goods, or jewels. In this fashion the lamas helped to maintain themselves but they also worked. Each was largely self-supporting according to his talents. Some were laborers, some household servants, stable boys, policemen, traders, students, teachers, doctors, business managers—all the types needed in a community that numbered three or four thousand. Each owned his own residence or rented a room from some wealthier inmate and so the usual hierarchy of talent and property prevailed.

Our guesthouse was located on level ground near the temples not far from the entrance—rather than on the hillside above where most of the lamas lived. It resembled those we had frequently stayed in during the trip, containing brick beds, or kangs, with small fireplaces or "stoves" built into them and flues to carry the heat throughout the bed. There were also braziers for cooking and warming tea. Perhaps the place had been cleaned once during the past hundred years. The stains where bedbugs had been mashed against the wall decade after decade gave the interior a speckled effect.

We spread our things on our beds and waited to see what would happen. I wanted very much to clean up. There had been little chance to do so during the trip and though I shaved daily (as usual in summer—in winter we let our beards grow as protection against the cold) by this time I was yearning for a hot bath. But no Tibetan bathes unless caught in the rain. I didn't want to attract attention by asking for a tub, so I heated water on a brazier and settled for a sponge-off.

I'd hardly finished it when an elderly lama appeared, clasped his hands, and after the usual bow and "God-be-with-you!" offered himself as my guide and mentor during my stay at Kumbum. This was a customary procedure at most large or famous lamaseries. He was comparable to the professional guides you find today at the Vatican in Rome or at the Acropolis in Athens. Like them this fellow made his living from the tourist trade.

Not far behind him came a young lama with what seemed a surprisingly prompt invitation to a meeting with His Holiness, the Tashi Lama. Putting on my hat I followed him to a simple dwelling not far away, not by any means a palace but a kind of private residence, flat-roofed, its walls plastered with a white lime sand, windbells at its eaves. Inside, seated on a low round dais, flanked by my Bogdo and two or three other shaved-headed lamas, was a man in early middle age with a quiet, friendly manner who greeted me cordially.

He wore a reddish purple robe of woven yak's wool embroidered with gold, red Russian leather boots with turned up toes, and the tassels of his yellow sash were decorated with turquoises. His rosary beads—108 of them, one for each book of the Tibetan bible—were also of turquoise. He was about my height and build and of a somewhat swarthy complexion.

While we chatted informally he expressed curiosity about my clothing. My hat interested him particularly. It was a center-crush Stetson such as the Canadian Mounties wore though its brim had been trimmed from four inches to three before it was sent me from the States. "Don't your ears get cold under a hat like that?" he joked, contrasting it to the usual Tibetan hat with earflaps. I said they would if I didn't change it for a Mongol cap with earflaps when winter came.

Kumbum Lamasery. (The Bodley Head, Ltd.)

Then we got down to business and Bogdo explained the purpose of our mission. His Holiness seemed fully informed as to what was going on in Mongolia, nodding several times but saying little. I described the military situation along the border and the kind of supplies our caravans were providing the Urga government. I said I thought an independent Mongolia was likely to receive strong support from such commercial interests as I represented, and perhaps from the U.S. government which approved movements toward independence as in the Philippines and elsewhere. In the end he gave no indication what he would do but suggested we meet again next day.

Two weeks went by. When not conferring with the God and his advisors I saw the sights of Kumbum with my lama guide. The most famous of these was the Tree of Faces, said to possess magic properties. One account said it grew from the hair of Tsong Khapa the reformer in whose honor the lamasery had been established. Another said it sprang from the blood shed upon the ground when his umbilical cord was severed at birth. At first the young tree didn't exhibit any remarkable characteristics but, later, pictures of Tibetan deities began to appear clearly outlined in its leaves along with the sacred formula: *Aum mani padme hum* which also appeared in its branches and bark, and all of this was the origin of the name Kumbum which means "hundred thousand images."

As time passed a considerable amount of disagreement developed over what its leaves and bark were supposed to reveal or actually did display. When the French priests Huc and Gabet saw it in the 1840s they were astonished to find upon each of its leaves not pictures but Tibetan writing of a green color, some darker, some lighter than the leaf itself. After examining the leaves carefully for fraud, Huc and Gabet decided that the writing appeared to be a natural portion of the leaf itself, as much as its veins and other substance. They also found that its bark and branches were similarly marked with written characters and that even when they peeled away the outer bark the underlying layer exhibited the outlines of these characters in germinating state!

The tree seemed to them to be very old, as it did to me, its trunk so big around three men joining hands could hardly have circled it. Its wood was reddish with a strong pleasing odor like cinnamon. It grew in an enclosure on the level area near one of the major temples and had broad leaves resembling those of a California maple or sycamore. I was told that by looking long and faithfully at its leaves you were supposed to be able to see, appearing in them, the faces of relatives you would meet during the coming year. In a region where family ties and tribal life were of paramount importance, this had wide appeal. The tree was surrounded by pilgrims staring reverentially at its leaves. To please my guide, I looked long and hard and said I thought

I saw the face of an old uncle, my nearest relative, who lived far away across the "big water."

The nearby Temple with the Golden Roof attracted my attention from the beginning. One day when there were not many people in evidence, I asked my lama to fetch me a ladder, ladders being in good supply, often used by the lamas to go from one flat-roofed level of their buildings to another. With its help I climbed to the roof of the temple ostensibly in awe and wonder but actually to apply a few drops of nitric acid to one of its tiles. Sure enough, the surface bubbled. It was solid gold plate.

There was plenty of gold in Tibet. You were apt to see parties of washers or panners, as they would have been called in the U.S., along the streams and you could pick it up in watercourses after a rain. But no central source or mother lode was known and though no mining was permitted in Tibet, we were always looking for that major vein. We former Alaskans were always dreaming of that "Asiatic Klondike," and a vial of nitric acid was a regular part of my equipment when in the field. Once a gold bug, always a gold bug.

I'd been waiting for an opportunity to speak to the God about the pyramids near Sian. Choosing a moment at the end of a meeting when we were sipping tea, I did so. Stirring the contents of his silver bowl daintily with his finger, he replied thoughtfully: "What did you think of them?"

"I think they're astonishing. Are they very old?"

"Our oldest books mention them as being old five thousand years ago." But "five thousand years" was a term often used loosely to mean simply "very old."

"Who built them?"

"We don't know. Men of ancient time. That's all we can say."

He asked if I would like to see some of his old books, and I accompanied him to a nearby building which housed the monastery library. Instead of standing upright on their shelves, its books were piled flatly according to size. Seated on the floor at low tables of blackwood were two or three lama librarians or scribes. He informed me they were inscribing the daily events of the monastery into a permanent record. They were writing on pieces of parchment with tapered camel's hair brushes. Now and then they

The Tashi Lama. (The Bodley Head, Ltd.)

rubbed the brushes on bars of India ink resembling bars of black soap. Other red-robed figures, seated at similar tables, studied books.

The Tashi Lama walked over to one of the shelves and picked up a large volume. It was bound in hide, tied with sinew, and looked very old. Opening it, he turned a few pages, saying they were the kind that recorded the existence of the pyramids and other ancient wonders. He held it out to me and I saw its writing: columnar, dim with age, apparently India ink, apparently an alphabet language resembling Mongolian. "We have even older records," he said, shutting the book and putting it back on its shelf.

Walking to a low table on which stood a large wooden box, he removed the lid and took out a clay disc about the diameter of an old-style phonograph record though somewhat thicker. Writing had been inscribed on it, apparently put there by a sharp instrument when the clay was wet. This writing too was columnar and was a kind of picture writing depicting humans, animals, and other natural objects interspersed with hieroglyphic symbols.

"We don't know exactly how old these are, perhaps ten thousand years," he explained, offering me the disc. Again he was using a figure I discounted, though convinced that the disc was extremely old. I declined to take it in my hands, fearing it might disintegrate.

"What does it say?" I asked.

"It tells of the dealings of our ancestors with a people far older who lived on land beyond the great water." He told me the ages-old story of a Tibetan Buddhist monk who sailed from China many years before Columbus discovered America, and came with his companions to the west coast of North America, particularly Mexico, which he accurately described. I had heard this account more than once along with later reports of junks which had drifted across the northern Pacific and come to our California coast on the Japanese Current. I hoped he would continue the subject but he didn't and I didn't think it wise to press him. As he replaced the disc, I noticed five or six more, and fragments of others, in the box.

Most lamaseries had libraries but this was the largest I ever saw, perhaps because Kumbum was a center for learning. It had colleges of botany, medicine, music, and many other arts and sciences including, as I discovered later, mysticism and the occult. Most lamaseries also had relic rooms, or museums, which contained a variety of strange or precious objects—old bones, fragments of pottery, sacred relics, coins, paintings, bowls of silver and gold, and statues. In one of them I saw a long thin-bladed sword resembling a rapier, which might have belonged to some European traveler in Marco Polo's time. There may have been such a museum at Kumbum but I didn't see it.

Despite a fear of giving offense, a blunt question led to my most remarkable experience at Kumbum. The Tashi Lama received information about the war in Mongolia with what seemed astonishing speed. In the course of our conversations, he would casually mention an event as having occurred a day or two before. Nearly 2,000 miles separated us from the fighting front. No telephone or telegraph lines connected Kumbum with the outer world. How did he get his information? Finally I asked him.

"Visit me this afternoon," he replied in his usual cordial way.

At mid-afternoon his runner escorted me to a building not far from his residence. Seated crosslegged on the floor in a semicircle on prayer rugs were a dozen or fifteen lamas apparently asleep. At least they were slumped in the manner they usually adopted when dozing in a sitting position. I saw three or four junior priests and lay brothers waiting watchfully in the background. The Tashi Lama stood with other senior lamas near the entrance door. There was absolute silence and an air of expectancy.

After about ten minutes one of the dozing figures stirred, stretched, yawned, opened his eyes, blinked and looked around in bewildered fashion as if not sure where he was. A lay brother hurried to him with a bowl of tea. He sipped it eagerly. Making a sign to me, the Tashi Lama walked over to him and I followed.

"Where have you been?" I heard the God inquire gently.

The lama replied slowly as if not yet fully awake: "I've been to Koko-tu-su."

I was astonished to hear him mention a place where I'd been myself a month or two earlier and where fighting might be in progress now.

"What did you see?"

"I saw Chinese infantry advance into the hills. The Mongols were waiting in ambush. Eighteen Chinese were killed or wounded. The Mongols escaped on fast horses."

"What else?"

"The Chinese are dragging cannon onto the plateau above Kalgan."

"How many cannon?"

"I saw four."

"What else?"

"That was all I saw."

"You have done well."

The Tashi Lama turned to me: "Now do you understand?" He chuckled, enjoying my perplexity as I shook my head. "It's very simple. He goes there. He sees. He comes back and tells us!" That was all the explanation he would give.

At the risk of offending, I returned to his intelligence center—or whatever it was called—on two later occasions. Finding myself well received, I took the liberty of examining one of the seated lamas as he was waking from what was probably a hypnotic trance. His forehead was cool, his pulse slow. His entire metabolism seemed depressed as it would be during sleep or hypnosis. When I asked what he had been doing, he shrugged and answered enigmatically: "Oh, I went there! I looked at things!"

A senior lama or the Red God himself was always present to hear these reports. What was happening? I cannot say exactly. Out-of -body travel or bilocation is something that may or may not be real. But certainly it has been talked about for a long time and the annals of China and India and those of the European Middle Ages are said to contain many instances of it. Even in my native California we had the legend of the Blue Nun, accepted as truth by the early Franciscan Fathers. She supposedly came flying from a monastery in Spain to minister to the heathen Indians and encourage the missionaries in their work. The annals of Tibet contain many supposedly authenticated instances of clairvoyance and out-of-body travel achieved by advanced practice of yoga. The practitioner's double or ethereal self is said to leave the physical body and accomplish various kinds of travel. Present day psychics insist this can be done, that we are really two selves, our substantive self and our insubstantial or astral self through which we are linked, more closely than we think, to all aspects of the universe. Most of us have personal knowledge of strange kinds of perception at a distance: intuitive awareness of a loved one's danger or death in a faraway place, location of lost children, a birth in the family, an extraordinary recovery of health, and so on. Perhaps what I saw at Kumbum was simply a highly developed aspect of this type of perception.

Within twenty or thirty seconds after waking from their hypnotic trance, the lamas involved were, as it seemed to me, back to earth. Clearly they had been in another state of consciousness.

Did the same observer "visit" the same locality during each "trip"? I could not be sure. Not knowing them, it was difficult to tell them apart, since they all dressed and looked very much alike, but I got the impression they worked in shifts and did not visit regions outside the Red God's spiritual domain, perhaps "went" only to places with which they were in some way familiar. I don't think they "visited" Peking, or New York, or London though they may have had the power to do so.

Did they read minds as well as see objects? There was no evidence that they did but perhaps they could have.

With a view to later corroboration, I made notes on what I heard reported. After I returned to Mongolia I showed my notes to people in a position to know of the events described in the Kumbum reports. Verification was absolute. In some cases, events were revealed to have occurred which my friends in Mongolia were not aware of.

After three weeks our negotiations at Kumbum came to what seemed a successful conclusion. Old Bogdo had a number of meetings with his brethren and probably with the Red God, too, which I did not attend, but in a final session where I was present the Tashi Lama suggested among other things that financial support for the Mongol revolt against China might be provided by lamaseries directly in the path of the fighting, and thus subject to looting. Coming from a supposedly unworldly spiritual leader, it seemed a remarkably practical suggestion. There seemed no question whose side he was on, though he made no outright commitment. We parted on best of terms. I said I would send him a center-crush Stetson and he said he would send me a Tibetan cap with earflaps.

When Bogdo and I returned to Mongolia we found a new spirit of unity. I never learned all that went on at diplomatic levels but for a while both Mongolia and Tibet enjoyed a substantial degree of autonomy—until the former was gobbled up by Russia and China and the latter by China alone, as will be seen.

I returned to the high country of west China and northern Tibet on several occasions but only once saw anything resembling what I'd witnessed in the occult center at Kumbum. Our party, which included T.A. Rustad, later Norwegian consul at Nanking, was following the bank of a deep, swift stream looking for a crossing place when we noticed a solitary lama approaching the opposite bank. The sight of a lone figure traveling cross-country in those regions where people usually traveled together and on established roads or trails was remarkable in itself. More remarkable was the way the man was walking. He seemed to glide or float a few inches above the ground.

Moving at a rapid pace, looking neither right nor left, he followed a course that would bring him to the stream some distance behind us, rather than opposite us where we might have had contact with him, which also seemed peculiar. We proceeded, however, glancing his way from time to time, and then without any of us noticing how it happened, he was on our side of the stream, proceeding on his course, looking straight ahead, paying us no attention whatever.

Supernatural? Maybe so. But experience was leading me to believe human beings capable of more things than I had dreamed possible as a younger man. Also I was becoming increasingly convinced that there is another world around us. Though we are able to penetrate this other consciousness only occasionally and sometimes by ways that seem strange, it is nevertheless there.

Not long after returning to Kalgan I received word from California that the Old Man, the tough old bachelor uncle who reared me, had died, which may have been one reason I didn't see his face in the leaves of the Sacred Tree. Quite seriously, the news severed a final bond with my old life and left me free for my new one. He had bequeathed me no legacy but perhaps the best one of all: independence and self-reliance.

J.W.G. Brodie and I (right) pose with some of the participants in the Chinese-Mongolian war of 1912/1915

4.

Siberian Tigers and Other Game

SINCE Kalgan was the principal gateway from China into Mongolia and the border region and could be reached easily by train from Peking, a number of foreigners came to see its sights. They inspected the huge arched gateway in the Great Wall through which our caravans passed and the much smaller gate adjacent, no larger than a bedroom door, the Gate of Sighs, through which for centuries exiles were banished into the barbarian wilderness.

They mingled with the life of our long colorful main street: its blacksmith shops, wheelwrights, leather workers, rope makers, hide and fur dealers, sing-song houses, a bank, ox carts and mule trains, feral dogs, stray pigs, and general tumult including occasionally a band of Mongol horsemen dashing by in picturesque costume. Sometimes these visitors went hunting antelope, gazelle or wolf on the plains above the town, and they often stayed with us since there was no other accommodation readily available for foreigners except the compounds of two or three trading firms like ours or the homes of a few missionaries.

J.A. Thomas came, always bringing gifts and a quiet sense of his own importance and that of B.A.T. affairs; and there were Singer Sewing Machine and Standard Oil men and members of the British and American diplomatic corps, including the intelligence officer at our American Legation in Peking, R.S. Clark, aforementioned. I became acquainted with Clark and he relied on us for some of his information. There were also soldiers, archaeologists, explorers, missionaries. A few years earlier Herbert Hoover, then a young mining engineer, had come to survey the mineral resources of the Kalgan region and to investigate the possibility of constructing a railroad across Mongolia, a project eventually carried out by Chinese and Russian Communists.

William Ashley Anderson, later a well known author, was my companion in Mongolia.

Hoover traveled by horseback to Urga where he found the Living God riding a bicycle madly around an inner court of the great lamasery. Later the God entertained him with Russian phonograph records.

Roy Chapman Andrews visited Kalgan en route to his "explorations" along the border and in Mongolia. Although he was pleasant enough, we always regarded Andrews as something of a Boy Scout who periodically left the comfort and security of the States to visit our frontier and had "adventures" which received a great deal of publicity, while we lived through the same sort of thing—and sometimes a good deal more—nearly every day as a matter of course.

However, such visitors enlivened our bungalow and kept us in touch with the outer world.

Left to ourselves on cold winter nights when the temperature fell to twenty below outside, we played checkers or poker, told stories, recited poems (my rendition of Kipling's *Oonts* or "The Commissariat Camel" becoming quite popular), or engaged in such indoor pastimes as boxing, wrestling, jumping from a standstill over the backs of upright chairs (try it some time), walking on your knees, extinguishing lighted cigarettes on your tongue, or biting pieces out of wine glasses. Young William Ashley Anderson had joined us fresh from New Rochelle, New York, where as a boy he had posed for the artist Frederic Remington, riding bareback through the wide doors of Remington's studio. Anderson quietly observed our antics and incorporated them later into imaginative stories which entertained a generation of *Saturday Evening Post* readers.

Practical jokes were staple entertainment. Once when a newspaper correspondent was visiting us, Anderson invited him into his room on some pretext. While they were there the telegraph key on the

Frans August Larson, honorary Duke of Mongolia, sits a female riding camel resembling my Ursha-Sahn. Larson, sometimes called the Prester John of the twentieth century, was a Swedish missionary, trader, and explorer who knew Mongolia and adjacent regions of China and Tibet better than anyone else. (F.A. Larson)

table began to click. Anderson answered and took down a message of banditry and bloody murder ostensibly coming from somewhere in the Mongolian wilds. Actually it was coming from the next room where I was operating my key.

Thinking he had a scoop, the correspondent wired the sensational story to his Peking paper. (Peking, Tientsin, Shanghai and Hong Kong all had English-language papers.) Next morning when we told him the truth it was too late to cancel his yarn, which made good reading when it appeared and was no more inaccurate than most others, the level of news reporting in the Far East being quite low.

For outdoor entertainment we rode bucking horses or played polo in our compound. Our balls were willow roots. The Mongols who watched us thought us far too gentle with each other, though as result of one collision Jim Brodie got pitched off on his head and turned black-and-blue down to his neck. The Mongols played their polo with a live sheep for a ball and nothing but mayhem for rules. As

Some Mongols from the western provinces were nearly nine feet tall. The man on the left is average size. This giant was sent by the Emperor of Mongolia as a present to the Czar of Russia.

many players as wanted to could participate. Their mallets were their hands. They snatched the poor sheep this way and that, forward passed him as you might a football, tore him limb from limb—never mind the squirting blood and guts—and whoever carried what was left of him across the line scored a goal. It was their national sport, perhaps older than the Indian polo we played, and was usually played between rival tribes or camps.

It reminded me in some respects of the rooster races held on the ranch at fiesta times, when the rider who successfully snatched a live rooster out of the ground was immediately surrounded by others who tried to take the bird away from him—the more blood, feathers, and confusion the merrier—while the crowd cheered.

Horse racing was another popular pastime with us, as it had been with me in California. Competing against the Mongols of the plains, we developed some fast horses that won good money on the Peking and Tientsin tracks where all the racehorses were Mongol ponies and the betting identical with our U.S. pari-mutuel system. Our Thamar, a roan gelding, set a track record at Peking by covering a mile in two minutes flat carrying 160 pounds.

We raced our camels in the wide-open country of the Mongolian Plateau, sometimes over distances of forty and fifty miles, wrapping ourselves beforehand in the bandage cloth previously described, unbleached muslin about six inches wide. It made you so stiff you had to be helped to your saddle like a medieval knight in armor. But once you were there you were really in place! All racing camels were virgin females around seven years old and most of the good ones came from the region west of Urga. They were as different from ordinary camels as race horses are from work horses, and each prince kept a separate herd of them as rich men do race horses in this country. A fast one must be among the fastest animals on earth over a long distance. Getting her started is the problem. For the first eight or ten miles you have to pound her with your stick and work at the reins attached to her nose pin until she finally understands you want a little speed. Then my Ursha-Sahn would run off and leave the fastest Mongol pony. At the end she would probably be doing a mile every three minutes, a pace she'd been holding for the last eighteen or twenty. But her stride measured twenty-one feet forward and nine feet from side to side, and would jar you to death if you weren't wrapped for it. On more than one occasion I ran a sixty-mile race for cash stakes, thirty miles out, thirty miles back.

Such activities, interspersed with periodic sojourns in Tientsin and Peking, added variety to our lives as we mingled with viceroys, living gods, bandits, and beggars, sometimes traveling as far afield as Shanghai and Hong Kong on business or holidays.

It was at this time that I got my nickname of Doc. Patching up my boys during hazardous caravan trips was routine but one especially momentous operation gave rise to what friends called my medical degree. There'd been a fight between two Mongol camps. A glancing bullet had smashed a young Mongol's ankle bone. He'd been that way ten days or more when they brought him to my camp, carrying him piggyback, the leg blue, green, yellow, and angry pink. The nearest doctor was about a thousand miles away in China. I shook my head inwardly. But the kid was smiling, game. I smiled back and explained to him and his father that with luck he might live if the foot were amputated. Otherwise he would in all probability die.

They talked it over. "Well, cut it off! How do you do it?"

I said: "It's quite a job. I've got no tools. I've got to make the tools. Besides, he'll be laid up for some time afterward, and you must promise to take care of him exactly as I say!"

They agreed.

I'd been thinking that the telegraph line was made of steel wire. Taking a heavy hunter's knife I stretched a piece tight and nicked it with the knife trying to hit with the same weight each time to make the nicks evenly spaced and the same depth. I strung it between two sticks and stretched a leather cord between the ends of the sticks to tighten the wire. When I tried out my saw on an antelope bone, it worked. I made a second in case the first got dull.

"Now we'll need four strong men!" I told them.

I had no anesthetic but my boys dug out the bottle of brandy. First I gave him six ounces, then doubled it, then waited five or six minutes and gave him another shot. Then we stretched him out flat on his back on the ground and pinned his arms and legs. One cut with the knife reached the bone. The blood flowed freely. I stopped it with a hot iron, searing it as you do a piece of steak. He was out by that time.

I'd cut into the upper calf where I could get meat to cover the bone afterwards. This wasn't like digging a bullet out of one of my caravan boys. I carried forceps for that job. Or a knife would do. Or if the bullet went clear through, I put carbolic acid on a rag and poked it through the hole on the end of a match stick, then took another piece of rag soaked with carbolic acid and left it in the wound to drain for a couple of days, then pulled it out, which ended the treatment.

I sawed on through and in a minute was done but when I got ready to sew up the meat it barely came together, no overlap, so I slit it higher to give more overlap so I could sew it and it would hold firm. Then I took my needles, one straight, one curved, about the size of sacking needles, and some thread and went to work. I sewed him up tight, soaked him in carbolic acid, bandaged him in clean rags, then put a sheepskin pad on the stump so it wouldn't catch cold.

About that time he came to and gave me a grin.

"You're a good patient!" I told him, giving him a pat. They took him back to their camp. I checked next day and things looked all right. I made them promise to dress the wound every fourth day as they'd seen me do. "When I come back I'll look at it again. If I find any dirt in it, you'll have a war with me!"

When I returned the stump was healed and they were carrying him around piggyback. "Will I grow a new foot?" he asked me.

"No, but it's better than being up there in the boneyard with the wolves chewing on you, isn't it?"

"Yes, but somebody has to carry me everywhere I go!"

"Ride a gentle horse, then. You've got the strength of your thigh and knee!"

When I came back three months later he was riding. I fashioned him a leg from soft wood. Soon he was riding everywhere with a stirrup to fit the peg. So I became known as "Doc" in Mongolia.

At the B.A.T. mess in Tientsin not long afterward, I was sitting down to breakfast with the gang, Hunter Mann, later an executive of Reynolds Metals, presiding, I taking considerable kidding because of my new nickname. We'd been at table a short while when Captain Pat Frissel, officer of the day, entered after depositing his side arms in the foyer, and began describing a riot of the night before which had nearly turned into a general uprising. All foreign troops in the Tientsin area had been alerted. But the Japanese had managed to control the situation without additional help. At this point I caught the eye of young William Ashley Anderson who was sitting opposite me and tipped him the wink.

The afternoon before from the fourth-floor windows of our mess on the Rue de France, Anderson and I had watched refugees streaming into the Foreign Quarter until they were stopped by our troops standing at barbed wire barricades. All north China was in a revolutionary uproar. Yuan Shih-kai, the old war dog and former Imperial Army Commander, was said to be bringing order out of chaos in Peking and to be in line for the presidency of the new Republic if Sun Yat-sen, who'd been named provisional president, resigned it, but we didn't see much order in Tientsin. Street executions were commonplace. Severed heads hung from lamp posts. Rifle fire crackled regularly.

The U.S. Fifteenth Infantry, later Ike Eisenhower's regiment, had arrived from the Philippines to join contingents provided by England, Germany, France, Russia, Italy, and especially Japan. It seemed that indeed another Boxer Rebellion was about to occur and again Tientsin would be a base for foreign military operations.

Fires licked above the city's rooftops in the late afternoon light. Mutinous troops were reported gathering downtown at the *yamen* demanding their pay. The prefect would probably make the usual explanation: though he had no money, he believed the local merchants would be willing to subscribe the necessary funds. That would be the signal. The mob would begin breaking into shops. Law-abiding citizens would close their shutters and take to their prayers.

It seemed too good a show to miss. Several of us including Anderson, C.W. Weeks, and Billy Christian who would join us later at Kalgan, made our way past our military patrols and headed for narrow, winding Old Clothes Street in the heart of downtown Tientsin.

Even under ordinary circumstances Old Clothes Street was like something out of the *Arabian Nights*. Its open-fronted shops displayed the furs of the snow leopard and Tibetan panda, Russian sable and ermine, Siberian tiger, incredibly large bear skins from Siberia and Kamchatka, jade from Tibet and lovely flowering shrubs made of multicolored gems. There were silk shops with distinctively musky smells; apothecary shops with precious medicinal herbs, ephedrine (*ma-huang*—excellent for asthma and bronchial disorders) and ginseng and aphrodisiacs made of unborn wapiti from Manchuria or rhino's horns from Southeast Asia; multicolored ceramics, delicately painted scrolls, embroidered screens, rare books. Crowds of people went about their business unconcernedly while disorder and violence threatened from some indeterminate source we tried in vain to discover.

As usual there was a bedlam of noises, the people shouting even in ordinary conversations as the Chinese do, parakeets squawking, pigeons cooing, long-eared black pigs running freely here and there, grunting and squealing and, with pariah dogs, acting as scavengers.

After wandering aimlessly and finding nothing very exciting, our party gradually broke up and I headed for a certain sing-song house on a quiet side street. Basically there were three classes of sing-song houses and they were not, contrary to popular belief in this country, houses of prostitution but places of entertainment and relaxation with a little romance thrown in under proper conditions. At the top were first-class houses like this one patronized by wealthy merchants, the military, and certain foreign visitors. Its girls had been acquired and carefully trained from infancy to be exactly what they were: accomplished companions who could play and sing, talk and joke, drink and gamble and, under the proper circumstances following an elaborate protocol of gifts and courtship, make love. The Chinese were extraordinarily formal and modest about such matters. I never saw them kiss in public or even hold hands. All that was for the bedroom. And there their techniques, ages old, perfected by long expertise, were probably second to none.

For the girls of a number-one house the early part of an evening was usually spent filling engagements at expensive restaurants where some rich man was entertaining his friends. Upper-class Chinese never entertained at home, always at restaurants, always with sing-song girls as guest entertainers and companions. Each girl sat beside or behind a male guest, to talk or sing, or gamble or drink with him as his spirit moved, with her *amah* or chaperone overseeing the whole proceeding with strict eye from a seat near the wall. Often the girls came and went in shifts at intervals by arrangement. A popular girl might attend eight or ten parties in one night. During the later part of the evening she was at home "receiving." When you arrived, you were ushered into a room where tea and watermelon seeds or tiny cakes were served. If you were a newcomer and hadn't made your selection, the girls passed in review before the open door and you made your choice. Then you observed further etiquette by inviting your friends, and her and other girls, to a series of parties over a week or ten days during which you singled her out by special but unobtrusive attention and gifts, a piece of jade, a gold bracelet. If she accepted and she usually did, in the end you and she remained alone after the party for a little personal talk.

Since I'd been in the field many long months and this was my night on the town, it seemed appropriate to me that I should be given exclusive use of the premises as general host, an inexcusable breach of etiquette which led to everything else that happened. Other patrons, notably a trio of Japanese Army officers, refused to see things my way. As consequence I felt compelled to begin ejecting them bodily. This was accompanied by no particular animosity on my part; it just seemed the appropriate thing to do. What was wonderful was the way the girls helped me. They had no particular love for these Japanese who treated them arrogantly as if they were concubines instead of inmates of a number-one house. Mama, who owned and managed them and the house, had no special love for the Japs either because they didn't pay their bills regularly, preferring to sign chits and forget about payment (though Mama, tottering here and there on her tiny bound feet, took care to stay out of sight during the ruckus I had aroused, so that she might be absolved of all responsibility for it later—she was indeed wise in the ways of the world). Her bound feet, incidentally, were not only status symbols but sex symbols. They were absolutely deformed and not more than four inches long. It was believed that they made a woman highly desirable—even though, as was the case here, she had to be helped or carried by one of her servants in order to walk more than a few steps.

During the heat of the melee I saw several girls using their personal needles. If you've never seen a sing-song girl wield her needle in close combat, you haven't seen all that a woman can do. Hers was not quite as long and rusty and crooked as the old-time sacking needles we'd used on the ranch, or the surgical needles I employed on my caravan boys, nor as long and rusty and crooked as the needles I sometimes used to sew a piece of hide to the foot of a lame camel to serve the animal as a shoe. But it would do. Clenched between first and second fingers, it stuck out of her fist like a hawk's claw.

The Japs who emerged into the street unscathed were fortunate. I caught a glimpse of the lowly doorman booting one in the behind as the spirit of fun spread.

Japanese plans for the subjugation of China were well advanced. They treated the Chinese like vassals and were cordially hated in return.

I'd enjoyed the proceedings greatly so far though I guessed what their consequences might be. Each night military contingents from the foreign legations patrolled the city to help the police maintain order and tonight was the Japs' turn. But at the moment Mama was serving me French champagne which sold in Tientsin for eleven dollars a case. Our party was going nicely when it was interrupted by a hubbub at the front door. A Japanese patrol was demanding admission.

Two minutes later the girls were helping me out a second-story window onto the roof of the adjoining building. After tender farewells I crept to the edge of the roof overlooking the street. Concealed by darkness, I peered over onto numerous helmets of numerous Japanese soldiers. The sight of those helmets gave me an idea. A twenty-pound roof tile landing on them might make them fit more snugly.

In the confusion no one could tell exactly where the tiles were coming from. A noisy crowd had gathered and the Japs began accusing the Chinese of tile throwing. So I tossed another and another.

By now I could hear soldiers ransacking the house behind me and knew that Mama's delaying tactics had been exhausted. So I departed across the rooftops tossing a tile now and then to keep things boiling in the street below, and by the time the soldiers emerged onto the roofs after me, I was well into the next block. It was no trick to jumped the narrow streets—they were only eight or nine feet wide—and the alleys were narrower.

My pursuers, however, handicapped by their short legs and military equipment, showed little taste for midnight broad-jumping at high level, and those who tried to follow on the ground were blocked by the crowd, while bedlam rose on every side. Pretty soon the Japanese forgot about me and got busy quelling the riot. When it had swept off across the city like a receding thunderstorm, I slipped quietly back over the rooftops to the sing-song house.

This time our party suffered no interruption. When sunrise came I began to think about how to get home safely. The authorities would be looking for me.

I discussed my problem with Mama. "Why don't you use my rickshaw?" she suggested. "It has curtains. I often travel with them drawn. You will not be stopped. The police know my rickshaw!" she said proudly. No doubt they did. And no doubt she paid them as much annually as any of Tientsin's leading merchants. A few minutes later I was on my way out of her compound in her rickshaw, sitting well back in one corner, curtains drawn, her shawl over my head, two boys pulling me.

At the main intersections native police, reinforced by American and Japanese soldiers, were keeping a sharp lookout. But they weren't looking for me in Mama's rickshaw.

When I reached the Queen's Hotel on Victoria Road, I removed my shawl and got out, paid the boys well, and went into the bar for an eye-opener, and then along to breakfast at our mess in the French Concession, passing the Rue de Chemin de Fer where the Western European and American prostitutes lived in style in their own homes with liveried servants, private carriages, and Paris clothes. I liked my style better.

Such escapades were the spice of our life and an expression of the times. They were also one reason why my account at the Hong Kong-Shanghai Bank in Peking was smaller than it should have been. In January 1913 we at Kalgan thought we might soon find ourselves in the path of a Mongol-Russian invasion of China that could rival or at least revive the memory of the famous ones by Jenghis and Kublai Khan. Anderson, our office manager, got a warning letter from Oscar Mamen who was minding the store alone in Urga.

Urga, Mongolia
January 8, 1913

W.A. Anderson, Esq.
B.A.T. Co.
Kalgan

Dear Mr. Anderson,

I have your letter of Dec. 7th also your wire and letter of Dec. 23rd for which I thank you. The cigarettes have not arrived yet, but I hope they will be here in due time as nothing has happened to caravans on that road as far as I know. If you have got candles for me in Kalgan, please forward same as soon as possible. The 500 cases candles, which arrived here on Dec. 25th, were sold out before sunset that day and now Urga is dark again. The road between Kalgan and Urga is reported to me as safe, but we know very little about the rest of the world here in Urga, so I can not guarantee anything in that line. I believe the time is not far off, when all transportation between Kalgan and Urga will be cut off because of a lot of my friends up here are preparing for a trip down to Kalgan and you will very likely see some gentlemen down there going about and knocking at peoples' doors with their Mauser pistols. We have had enough of these people here and shall be glad to get rid of them. Mr. Larson left Urga for Kalgan yesterday with a big cartload of dogs [a code word for furs or silver]; he will be in Kalgan in 20 days if he does not freeze too much in the Gobi. I am quite alone here now and do not see other people than Mongols, Burriats, Russians and other rot. What is to become of our business here in the future, I really do not know. I have asked the Living God about the future but he did not know much more than anybody else. At present everything is peaceful here. My best wishes for a happy new year.

Very sincerely,
O. Mamen

The letter, mailed in Urga, went by pony express to Verkne-Udinsk in Siberia, thence by rail along the Trans-Siberian and Chinese Eastern to Peking, thence also by train to Kalgan where it reached us amid a flurry of panicky inquiries from Peking as to the true state of affairs on the border. Were the Mongol Hordes really approaching? Was the Great Wall once again under siege? The fantasy nightmare of Chinese rulers then as now was of a united belligerent Mongolia backed by powerful Russia sweeping over those 150 not very long miles between Kalgan and Peking—sweeping over not only one but two or three great walls, there being several inner loops and spurs between the true or outer wall and the Chinese capital.

After finding out all he could about the local situation, Anderson in turn reported calmly to Billy Christian, our Peking manager.

Kalgan, January 16, 1913

Dear Chris,

You may put down any report of Russian troops being in Kalgan at the present time as false. That much I know; but as to any information of troops approaching from the north, I am afraid I cannot help you.

Strange to say, our knowledge of events in Mongolia is very slight, and the most we know is that the majority of reports in the Tientsin and Peking papers concerning affairs here are wrong. I think it probable that Cossacks have moved into Inner Mongolia, and certainly a great many Chinese soldiers have gone *out* of Kalgan, and up to the plateau, with mountain guns, automobile transports, and all munitions.

Larson, who is returning now from Urga across the Gobi, has written to Mrs. Larson here that war is apparently inevitable; and that the Mongols are reviving their ancient fanatic belief that they are predestined conquerors. Russian officers are drilling large bodies of Mongol troops in Urga; but recently, when some foreigners attempted to photograph them, all cameras and equipment were seized by the Russians and confiscated. As Mr. Larson is desirous of not having his name connected even remotely with Mongolian affairs, I hope you will not mention his name unnecessarily in this connection; but you may be sure that whatever he says on the subject is probably more authoritative than the opinion of any other foreigner in the East. I expect to get some more explicit information from him as soon as he arrives.

Several Chinese soldiers were recently executed here for highway robbery, and some of our dealers report that countrymen are not coming to town to purchase for fear of soldiers and fighting, but as far as I can ascertain everything is as quiet as can be expected.

No local preparations have been made for the defense of Kalgan, and if it becomes necessary to fight to keep it, the fighting will probably all be on the plateau around Hunorfsas . . .

Give my bestest to Ki . . .

Very Sincerely,

W.A. Anderson

Things smouldered on, rumor succeeding rumor, skirmish, skirmish, banditry and freebooting flourishing, until at last Frans August Larson decided to take matters into his own hands.

The big Swede, tall and blond as a Viking chieftain, was outstanding wherever he went. Everyone who knew him, Chinese, Mongol, foreigner respected him. His reputation as a man of peace, fairness, and strength too, was legendary. Once when an ugly mob of looters threatened to attack his missionary church compound, he walked out the front gate, picked up their leader and threw him in a mud puddle, which doused the mob's fiery ardor as well.

Larson had come to Mongolia as a young man walking all the way from Peking to the border and for years wandered alone among the Mongols with a little caravan of horses and camels, peddling Bibles and preaching the word of God to the inhabitants of the Gobi and beyond. Now he was not only the confidant of the Living God at Urga but of Yuan Shih-kai, president of China. Yuan had asked him to make peace with Mongolia. Larson went to Urga. He talked to the Hutukhtu but to no avail. Most of the Mongols doing the fighting were from the border provinces and the God had little direct control over their nomad princes. Accordingly Larson who spent summers at his camp at Tabo-ol on the high plains some ninety miles northwest of Kalgan decided to act on his own.

He rode to the camp of the principal Mongol leader not far away. He'd known Prince Na for many years. They trusted each other. As they reclined side by side on a brick bed sipping tea—pistols within reach because you never knew what might happen or who was loyal to whom and the bed was in a Lama temple Na had recently occupied—Larson said quietly to the nomad chieftain: "It's foolish for Mongolia which already has its independence to continue this war. What do you stand to gain? China would be of no use to you even if you should conquer it."

After a sip of tea, Na agreed. "Yes, what would we do with China? Who would wish to live in such a filthy, unhealthy place!"

Larson pressed this point, knowing how the free living Mongols of the open spaces loathed the crowded lowlands of China. He reminded Na of the numerous Mongols who'd gone to China to attend festivities at the court of their Manchu cousins and died there. "Why don't you stop this war? If you set the example, other princes will follow."

Na replied it was very difficult to stop a war once it got started. "Besides, what guarantee have we the Chinese won't invade us if we cease hostilities?"

Larson said he had Yuan Shih-kai's promise that whatever terms he, Larson, agreed on would be honored. "The Chinese forces will withdraw. I'm authorized to say that China will pay all the expenses of your men as they travel back to their homes and also pay for the damage the Chinese army has done to Mongolia."

What finally turned the trick was Larson's offer—incongruous considering his friend's previous statement about living in China—to make Na and 200 of his men Yuan Shih-kai's personal bodyguard. "President Yuan is eager to have a personal guard composed of 200 valiant Mongols whom I shall recommend."

Like many a simple hearted Mongol before him, Na was flattered by the idea of lording it around the court at Peking, and it tickled his sense of the ridiculous to think that he would be guarding the man he had recently been fighting against. He agreed to choose 200 men and go to Peking if Larson would go with him.

It was arranged, and though not all the princes followed Na's example and the war continued to be very real for some of those including ourselves who were exposed to it firsthand, Na and his men turned up at the Royal Palace in Peking where they soon became an outstanding tourist attraction.

What had really happened behind the scenes was this: Russia and China had agreed secretly that Russia would withdraw its support for Mongolian independence and accept the autonomy of Outer Mongolia under Chinese suzerainty.

This nice little double cross became official with a treaty signed at Kiakhta on the Siberian border in June of 1915 to which the unsuspecting Mongols were a party. Of course they had no knowledge of the secret understanding between Petrograd and Peking, and they probably had considerable difficulty reading the fine print of the treaty itself, since such diplomatic niceties were not their strong point.

So they were taken advantage of and sold down the treacherous river.

Russia had a sudden compelling interest in an accommodation with China: World War I which was occupying nearly her full attention and causing her terrible losses, and she wanted not only a friendly China at her rear but possible Chinese aid against the Central Powers.

After the war the Russian Communists repudiated the secret understanding with China and encouraged Mongolian autonomy under Russian influence, thus repaying the Chinese in some of their own coin.

While formal hostilities between Mongols and Chinese subsided, thanks largely to Larson, freebooting and banditry along the border continued unabated.

Once Mamen and I rode 200 miles into the Gobi to meet the Suchow caravan and escort it safely across the border. It originated in far western Kansu some 1,500 miles distant. Suchow was at the western end of the Great Wall, west of Kumbum in the region called the Kokonor, on the Old Silk Road that ran up there from Sian and Lanchow and passed obliquely to the northwest into Sinkiang, also touching such market towns as Hami and Urumchi. Bandits preyed on its traffic throughout. They'd usually attack the rear of our trains, usually at dawn just as we were coming to the end of a night's march, tired, ready to halt and unload. They'd hit us with a Wild Indian charge, yelling and firing, trying to stampede and drive off the last eight or ten camels. But usually our outriders would give the alarm in time and the boys and Mu-Yan would immediately *dzuk* all camels down, including their own riding ones, and get down prone behind their mounts with rifles ready and active while we on horseback converged as fast as we could and usually prevented any loss or, after hot pursuit, recovered any camels and loads that had been taken.

A lot of lead flew but seldom was anyone killed. I got a nick across the bridge of my nose which, my friends said, added distinction to my appearance.

My "Black Horse Troop" of Mongols patrolled the China-Mongolia border against bandits and freebooters. I'm on the gray at left.

Another time at Pao-tou-chen near the Yellow River, my men and I became targets of opportunity for several hundred mutinous and trigger-happy Chinese soldiers. Luck got us through safely. Not for nothing were we officially known as B.A.T.'s Frontier Division as though the corporation were an army and we its shock troops.

In self-defense, I organized what became known as the Black Horse Troop. It consisted of twenty of our best men—Mongol means "brave man"—all of them mounted on distinctive black ponies, I on a white one. Together we patrolled the border north and south of Kalgan, escorting caravans and keeping order generally.

Sometimes, in these and related activities, I used the Dodge touring car with collapsible top Thomas had bought me, he thinking it would enable me to make better time than with ponies or camels, and maybe make a fast getaway from bandits, but it was usually out of order or out of gas, and when I wrecked it during a wolf hunt I gave it up, preferring ponies and camels anyway.

Wolf hunting was a continuous occupation of the Mongols on the plains in which we joined, wolves being a constant menace to their flocks and herds. They seldom wasted bullets on a wolf, preferring to ride it down and kill it with a blow on the head from a steel stirrup or wooden club. They had more fun that way.

Sometimes they "hawked" wolves using black eagles as falcons. The eagles would fly at the heads of the running wolves, bewildering them with flapping wings and striking talons until the riders caught up.

The Mongols also hunted antelope (there were no pronghorned antelope in Mongolia, all were single-horned) and gazelle in organized fashion, driving them into nets, and selling them to Chinese merchants. Railroad cars stacked high with their frozen carcasses were a common sight at Kalgan in late fall and winter. Frozen pheasants, too, went by the hundreds of thousands to Peking and other markets.

Before I leave the subject of wolves I should say a word about Larson's experience with them. Prester John, as we called the big tall Swede after the legendary Christian Bishop of Asia, was coming home to Kalgan from Urga one snowy December in *his* Dodge touring car at a speed of all of fifteen miles an hour following ruts in deep snow. More snow was falling and through it he heard, above the noise of the engine, the howling of wolves. Looking back he saw about forty strung out in hot pursuit of him and the Dodge. These were the big brownish black wolves of the subarctic forests and plains and would weigh up to 130 pounds. For wolves to attack humans was not uncommon in China and Mongolia and it usually occurred like this in winter when the animals were hard-pressed for food. But the humans were usually afoot, not in a motor car. They were gaining on him rapidly, Larson could see. It was impossible for the Dodge to go any faster through the heavy snow so he told his Chinese driver to hold her steady in the wheel ruts while he climbed into the back seat. The canvas top was down, folded along the rear of the seat, and steadying his hands on it he began to fire at the oncoming pack with his Colt revolver. He knocked over the big leader who wasn't more than a few good bounds away, so close he could see its red tongue lolling out hungrily, and the others immediately leaped upon their fallen chief and began tearing him limb from limb. When Larson knocked over another they treated him likewise.

He downed a third which the ravenous pack also stopped to devour and this gave him time to pull away to a distance of a hundred yards or more. There he told his driver to stop and taking his Winchester he downed a half dozen more from that distance. These the others also devoured, and while they were doing that Larson drove on his way and after crossing the Gobi arrived safely back in Kalgan for Christmas.

Some of the game along the border was rare and unique and much sought after by collectors as well as market hunters. Up in Manchuria, for example, were the blackcock, or black grouse, the gorgeous blue-black males weighing up to twelve pounds, the drab gray females six, and neither found anywhere else in the world, so far as I learned, except northern Scotland and some parts of western Europe. Also in Manchuria were the increasingly rare and valuable musk deer, small and hornless. The males had needle-like fangs—eyeteeth prolonged—with which they struck when fighting. A gland under their bellies near their genitals contained the dark viscous musk which formed the basis for many perfumes. Its scent was supposed to be more penetrating than that of any other known substance.

These were the great days of specimen collecting by museums and zoos and one of our leading collectors was a slim, soft-spoken Englishman born in China of missionary parents. Arthur de Carle Sowerby had been educated in England and made his way back to China via Canada where he'd worked as a cowboy, which gave us something of a common background. During his expedition with Clark through Shensi and Kansu, Sowerby had seen the large burial mounds near Sian including a very large one said to be the tomb of the mythical Yellow Emperor, thought to have lived as early as 2700 B.C. but none exactly resembling the pyramids I'd seen. Later Sowerby became prominent as founder and editor of the *China Journal of Science and Arts* and wrote several books.

Now, using Kalgan as his base, he was field-collecting for the British and Smithsonian Museums.

Together we went down into the mountains toward Kuei-hua-cheng for argali, the largest of all the wild sheep, and got one head with horns that measured twenty inches around at the butt and forty-eight on the curve. (When rams like that fought during the mating season you could hear the sound of their collisions for several miles on a still day and their necks were nearly devoid of hair as result of such impacts.) We went up into the Imperial Forest below Lama Miao for the high-flying Reeves pheasant which has a tail four to six feet long but is only half the size of the common ringneck, and we made several trips out along the Chinese Eastern and Trans-Siberian railways after bear, boar, and tiger, and into central and western China for the gray goral and golden takin. But the rarest specimen we hunted was the milu or Père David's deer. The milu became known to the western world back in the mid-1800s when an enterprising French priest and amateur zoologist, Father Armand David, peered over the wall of the Imperial Hunting Park at the outskirts of Peking and saw a sight which astonished him. It was a strange looking creature, nearly four feet high at the shoulders, covered with long reddish hair. It had the horns of a deer, the beard of a goat, the feet of an ox, and the tail of a donkey. It was the legendary semi-sacred milu or "*ssu-pu-hsiang*," the "four in one." The Imperial Hunting Park was off limits to everyone but the emperor and his retinue who hunted there, but Father David's zoological zeal was not to be denied. He waited his chance, bribed the Mongol soldiers who guarded the park and acquired a couple of skins which he sent to a prominent authority in Paris who named the species after him. Milus were depicted in cave drawings and ancient Chinese tapestries and in popular storytelling. Until 1900 several remained alive in the Imperial Hunting Park, where they had been propagated for many years. During the looting and burning which accompanied the Boxer uprising they disappeared. After peace was restored a search was made so that the species might not be lost, but none had been found.

Sowerby and I were continuing that search. A milu dead or alive would be a collector's triumph and extremely valuable.

Beginning with the marshy areas of north China which they were supposed to have inhabited, we traveled hundreds of miles tracking down reports, talking to people in various parts of the country who claimed to have seen milus (always many years ago) but we never found one and neither did anyone else and the species passed into extinction so far as we knew.

Another creature, stranger even than the milu, was constantly in our minds when we went to the Far West. He was the humanoid "hairy wild man" or "wild bandit" (*jen-huza*, the Mongols called him)

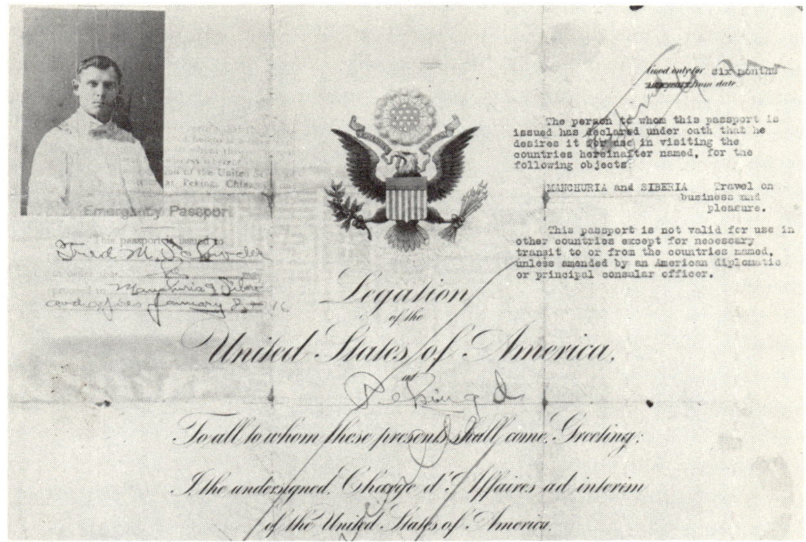

Emergency Passport

Good only for six months from date

The person to whom this passport is issued has declared under oath that he desires it for use in visiting the countries hereinafter named, for the following objects:

MANCHURIA and SIBERIA Travel on business and pleasure.

This passport is not valid for use in other countries except for necessary transit to or from the countries named, unless amended by an American diplomatic or principal consular officer.

Legation of the United States of America, at Peking

To all to whom these presents shall come, Greeting:

I the undersigned Chargé d'Affaires ad interim of the United States of America

This passport enabled me to collect animal and bird specimens in Manchuria and Siberia for the British and Smithsonian Museums.

Arthur Sowerby (right) and I with some of our trophies.

of Mongolia and northern Tibet, perhaps a northern cousin of the *yeti* we have heard so much about in recent years. He was said to be covered with hair or dressed in animal skins worn with hair side out. William Rockhill, the American missionary explorer, away back in the 1880s put together a description of him from reports as: "covered with long hair, standing erect, and making tracks like men's." Supposedly he lived in caves far above snow line or in the loneliest parts of the deserts. He subsisted on berries, grass seeds, marmots, rabbits, the markhor (or elusive wild goat with the high, spiraled horns), wild sheep, wild camel (bands of wild camel still roamed the northern Tibetan highlands), wild ass, or yak. From time to time villagers found a domesticated yak with head smashed in and body ripped to pieces, evidence of the *jen-huzas'* ferocity and strength, and sometimes lonely herdsmen disappeared or their bloody remains were found.

Reports differed as to whether the wild bandits possessed weapons. Some claimed they used bone-tipped spears and arrows and bows of bone. Others insisted they were simply large apes that might have been seen with a stick or rock in hand. Opinions differed, too, as to whether they possessed fire but all agreed they could be lethal when provoked and should be strictly avoided. In one of my trading trips deep into northern Tibet and western Sinkiang we were crossing an eighteen-thousand-foot pass with yaks as pack animals when my Mongol hunters reported seeing such a creature standing upright at a great distance, but that was the closest I ever came to seeing one. And I suspected maybe they were "seeing things," while at the same time I tended to believe the folklore of the subject which has since proven substantially true.

A Tibetan hunter we talked to gave us what he claimed was a firsthand description of meeting a hairy wild man. He was out after snow leopard, a premium skin, at an elevation of about eighteen thousand when he saw what he thought was a bear standing upright and watching him from a distance of about three quarters of a mile across a small valley. The "bear" was standing motionless in a patch of snow. It held what appeared to be a stick or spear in its right hand. Scared stiff but curious, the hunter stayed motionless too. They faced each other that way for several minutes. Then the bear turned and, remaining upright, walked off across the snowfield and disappeared among some rocks.

Though normally he lived in fear and trembling of such creatures, the hunter claimed that curiosity got the better of him on this occasion—since the wild man seemed clearly bent on not making his acquaintance—and he cautiously worked his way around the head of the little valley until he came to the snow patch where the creature had been standing. There he saw the tracks. They were about half again as large as those made by a normal man. Judging from the length of his strides the wild man must have been over seven feet tall, the hunter said, take it or leave it. Because there was a crust on the snow and each step had broken through it leaving an indistinct outline, he could not distinguish heel and toes clearly. He followed a short distance till the trail became lost in rocks, and then deciding discretion to be the better part of valor, turned back.

While retaining my ties with B.A.T., I became increasingly an independent trader, buying and selling for other firms—skins and furs mostly, mostly for Wilson & Company of Tientsin, some of whose principals I'd met years earlier in London. I received a commission of four percent, two for everything I sold, two on everything I bought. I also guided representatives of U.S. firms on prospecting trips, men like G.T. Bridgman, field representative for the Guggenheim brothers (Daniel, Isaac, Murray, Simon, Solomon, founders and owners of the American Smelting and Refining Company which had acquired the fabulous Kennecott Copper Mine or "Big Bonanza" in Alaska while I was employed there) and Harry Putnam, representing U.S. Steel, which had its eye on China's resources as did many big American corporations. These field trips took me from the Siberian to the Indochina borders and to the interior province of Hunan, where the ever-industrious ever-ingenious Chinese piped natural gas into their homes for heat and light entirely by bamboo pipes. The giant bamboo threaded easily and may be said to have been the forerunner of our nonmetallic pipes of today. With similar ingenuity they produced high quality antimony. They heated crude ore in open clay pots to drive off the volatile components containing the antimony which was condensed on wires strung above the pots in large sheds and easily collected. Every first-rate miner, incidentally, made his own powder, just as every professional hunter did. Tom didn't use Harry's and Dick didn't use Jim's. They were very particular about it. The secret of making it was handed down from father to son. And

I purchased a great many skins and furs at Hailar in Manchuria for Wilson & Company of Tientsin. Here I oversee the baling of several thousand of them, flanked at either hand by the local dealers from whom I purchased them.

the other fellow's was always considered inferior. It was coarse black powder but they used it with extraordinary skill.

In Manchuria again, I was looking over iron ore prospects north and east of Mukden in dense hardwood-forest country when I ran across fresh tracks of a wild pig herd. The pigs were after hazelnuts and ginseng root, the ginseng with its low broad leaves still being found in natural state despite its great value and consequent intensive harvesting for drug use. A so-called "perfect" root in the shape of "the little man"—that is, forked with arms and legs—could bring you $400 an ounce at Canton, the drug center of the Orient. The three-to-four-inch-long roots were also cultivated secretly, harvested late in the fall, macerated for several days in fresh water, then dried until hard and translucent. Ground up and added to tea, they were highly prized as a general tonic and aphrodisiac.

Following the pigs, I was careful to stay down wind. Once they wind you, silence falls and they disappear, and all that you hear is the blue whiskey jacks jeering from a nearby limb. If you hear a pig squeal, better choose your tree, because here, likely, comes the whole herd and they will mean business.

Manchurian pig herds produced the finest commercial bristles for brushes and also some very large boars weighing up to 500 pounds. When I noticed a track that could have been made by a yearling calf, my expectations began to rise. I could hear the pigs talking to each other a few yards ahead of me and smelled the pungent odor of freshly uprooted earth. Engrossed in my hunt, oblivious to everything else, I reached a clearing overgrown with hazelnut bushes, exactly the kind of place where a boar might linger at the rear of a herd. I edged out into it, rifle ready—but not ready for what happened.

There was a flash of orange from what seemed almost under my feet as an enormous tiger jumped up and trotted off with stiff-legged strides. I was too astonished to react until he'd almost reached the trees. My snap shot had no visible effect and I felt sure I'd missed him completely.

The Siberian or Manchurian tiger was and is the largest of the big cats. He outweighs the African lion and weighs nearly twice as much as his Chinese, Indian and Borneo cousins. He is more vividly marked than any of his relatives and his hair is much longer. He was little known to the western world until the construction of the Trans-Siberian Railroad through his territory in the 1880s and '90s, when his depredations became so severe that Russian troops were assigned to protect Chinese construction workers. It's one of the few cases when a nation's troops were deployed against wild animals. The tigers just seemed to resent human encroachment into their habitat. Or maybe because of their large population they welcomed the arrival of a new food supply. But I seriously think that animals are much more sensitive to invasions of their territory than we realize. At Tsavo in British East Africa lions staged regular attacks on railway workers on the Mombasa-Nairobi line and actually brought construction to a halt. And in our part of California in early days, mountain lions became so depredacious that when Indian women went down to the creeks to wash clothes, men with rifles accompanied them. The atmosphere of the times may have had something to do with it. Our back country was still wild. It still belonged primarily to wild creatures. Man was an intruder. And the animals knew it. The same may have been true at Tsavo and along the Trans-Siberian Railway in the 1890s.

By the early 1900s the Siberian was one of the most sought after big game trophies, and Sowerby and I had looked in vain for one out along the Trans-Siberian as far as Lake Baikal, the western limit of his range. Now one could have had me for breakfast. There was no guarantee, of course, that he was a man-eater, but in that country you never knew.

My chance to get even came, or was thrust upon me, a few months later. With Bridgman I was fifty miles north of the Amur River in Russian territory looking for gold prospects. Entering Siberia was no problem then. You simply went to the nearest Russian ministry or consulate, had your passport stamped, got a letter of introduction and went in.

The country north of the Amur was rolling grassland interspersed with patches of forest and an occasional rimrock, like parts of Arizona. We'd pitched camp late one afternoon by a spring near the base of a rocky bluff. While the boys turned the stock out to graze and got things ready for supper and Bridgman relaxed on his bedroll, I picked up my geologist's hammer and strolled over to see what minerals the nearby bluff contained. I didn't think of taking a gun. I was going only about 150 yards from camp.

I'd knocked off a piece of rock and was sitting on a small boulder at the base of the bluff examining it through my magnifying glass when I heard a pebble fall from above. Turning my head carefully, I looked up. There in full sunlight on a ledge twenty-five feet above me were the head and shoulders of an enormous tiger. The light set off his vivid markings and his extraordinarily long hair so that he seemed absolutely monstrous. I was terrified half out of my wits until I realized he wasn't looking at me but at the camp. The activities there—pans rattling, boys calling to one another—were engaging his attention. A slight change in the wind, however, even a chance glance down, might make him aware of me, although I was fortunately in the shadow which had begun to accumulate at the base of the bluff. I didn't dare breathe deeply or even look directly at him again for fear of giving myself away, and remained absolutely motionless, rock in one hand, magnifying glass in the other, watching him out of the corner of my eyes while waiting further developments.

They weren't encouraging. The head and shoulders of a second tiger, slightly smaller, had appeared beside the first. It was probably his mate. Her attention also had been attracted by the activities of the camp. I wondered if they were reconnoitering for an attack on it as the tigers along the railroad had attacked construction camps in earlier days. Heightening my wonderment, a third tiger appeared. He was considerably smaller than the first two, probably last year's cub. Two more followed, much smaller, this year's kittens. Then I had five Siberian tigers hanging over me, and I was caught quite literally between a rock and a hard place.

Should I stay still and hope they didn't come any closer? Should I jump up and shout in hopes of frightening them off? Should I run for camp?

Without warning the big fellow vanished. The others followed suit in order of their appearance. I broke all records for the 150-yard dash. Long before reaching camp I was shouting at the *mafoos* to bring the horses because we were going to chase tigers.

We galloped after them for two or three miles across the rolling grassland but caught a clear view only once, all five loping along in the last light of the sun, before they entered some trees and disappeared.

Tigers behave in strange ways. Most cats hate water but tigers don't mind it. I've known them to swim the Amur when it was choked with blocks of floating ice. Near Hong Kong they swam regularly between the mainland and offshore islands; from time to time fishermen killed them a mile or more at sea. They will live in close proximity to humans and never harm them. One had kittens in the Shwe Dagon Pagoda in Rangoon when a friend of mine was there. Yet they took our U.S. soldiers from guarded camps during the Korean War. So they carry on an unpredictable relationship with Homo sapiens.

In 1916 I was in Manchuria on business again and was thinking of the tigers that had bested me every time I'd encountered them so far. Accordingly I talked to Charles K. Moser, our U.S. consul at Harbin. Moser, always helpful in business matters and a sportsman besides, suggested I talk to the district manager of the Chinese Eastern Railway, a Russian who was also a tiger hunter. He in turn informed me that the tigers were moving south because of a cholera epidemic which had decimated the pig herds, their chief food supply, and recommended that I try the Korean border area. He furnished me a letter of introduction and a courtesy pass and I rode the Russian train with my two boys through beautiful hardwood forests of oak and walnut down toward the Korean line. They were burning that fine hardwood in their locomotives though there was plenty of coal in the country.

At a point where a narrow gauge joined the main line we got off and took the narrow gauge back into the forest to a camp where coolies were cutting and cording walnut and oak under direction of a burly young Russian superintendent. Before our first bottle of vodka was empty he was telling me about the opium outlaws who lived deep in the woods and played hide-and-seek with the tigers. He would send out inquiries; within a few days one of them would bring us word. And meanwhile here was some more vodka.

A day or two later a ragged emaciated Chinese appeared in camp. He wore a frayed bit of blue cloth, his head and feet were bare and his hair was pieced out with string to comply with the old law requiring every man to wear a pigtail. News of the revolution and the law's repeal hadn't apparently penetrated to these parts; or if it had, like many others he preferred to keep his pigtail, having worn it all his adult life. Our conversation went like this.

"Master, a tiger was in my poppy patch last night!"

"Where is he now?"

"Not far. He killed a rascally pig that was uprooting my poppies and dragged it into the underbrush. I think he's still there!"

"How far from here?"

"Six *li*."

"Do you know this tiger?"

"Oh, yes! At night when he prowls outside I sit in my house and pull strings to rattle the noisemakers in my poppy patch, and I light firecrackers to frighten him, but he does not go away. He's a *day-yan* [a bad one]. He eats the Long Pig [man]!"

"Have you friends who can help us?" Beaters might be needed.

"They are eagerly waiting!"

He led me and my boys through thick woods to a clearing where his log-sod hovel stood and his opium poppies were blooming. Though the production and use of opium were banned throughout China it was in such demand that its illegal cultivation was widespread, and since Manchurian or black opium brought the highest price, our friend could make a nice living if he didn't consume too much of his product himself, which, judging from his gaunt yellow look, he was in danger of doing; or if the *yamen* runners didn't catch him. The runners might reduce his ankle bones to pulp by repeated tappings with their sticks, so that he could never walk again except to hobble. Or they might put him in the stocks, standing on a pile of boards, and remove one board each day until he almost but not quite hung by his wrists and neck and almost, but not quite, choked or died of thirst or starvation. The Chinese principle of justice was simple. It was always to make the punishment a little worse than the crime. For serious infractions The Punishment of the Thousand Cuts was still in use. Your body was encased in a metal jacket resembling a jacket of mail. The jacket was tightened by a key until your flesh protruded through the meshed links. The flesh was sliced off flush with the metal by a razor or sharp knife. Then you were released. No doctor could treat you or friend help you without risking death, because you bore the official taboo of The Punishment. You soon died, your body a mass of suppurating sores.

His opium poppies were a beautiful sight against the background of green woods. They were predominantly red, blue, and white, waist high. Every day during the harvest season in late June, a few weeks hence, he would make a spiral incision in each poppy pod which allowed a drop of milky fluid to collect at its bottom, and every day he would go around with a bottle and collect that drop of opium. He would sell it to black-market dealers who would see that it reached the ten to fifteen million Chinese addicted to the drug. The authorities had been trying for years to control the use of opium. Just when they were on the point of succeeding, the British, in one of the most unconscionable acts the British ever committed, in my opinion, forced them to accept a huge quantity of Indian opium. It was the kind of thing that started the infamous Opium War of the mid-nineteenth century which resulted in China's ceding Hong Kong to the British and in the whole sorry system of foreign encroachment on Chinese sovereignty—and in the addiction of millions of people. British dealers had recently pressured the Chinese into accepting some 3,000 chests of opium valued at about $20 million.

The swath the tiger had made through the poppies while dragging the pig away was plain. We followed it until it entered the trees. There two more opium outlaws were waiting. They resembled our guide in appearance and were armed with stick rattles and tin cans containing rocks for noise-making. They assured me in hushed tones that the tiger was nearby but that with their expert assistance we should have no trouble killing him. His carcass would be a rich reward for them. They could sell it to the apothecaries who would convert it—flesh, blood, bone—into valuable medicine. The Chinese believed in sympathetic therapy. A potion containing powdered tiger bone or dried tiger blood was supposed to give you the courage of a tiger, just as one containing crushed wapiti horns was supposed to make you more virile.

By now it was nearly noon and hot. There was no wind to speak of, only treacherously veering air currents that came from no particular direction. The light, too, was deceptive, When the leaves stirred, they cast a shifting pattern on the undergrowth. It was the kind of light in which a tiger's coat makes ideal camouflage.

The flies were thick but I was glad of that. Flies can be helpful when you are stalking a tiger by daylight.

After a few yards his trail disappeared into a large patch of brush containing a few scattered trees. Taking my .450 double-barreled express, I started around it, leaving the others where they were, and after making a circle of half a mile or more and finding no outgoing sign, I decided he must be in that brush patch. When a tiger has eaten he usually sleeps. With luck I might surprise him.

I'd hunted tigers successfully in south China and in the central and southwestern provinces, and once during a visit to Indochina and knew something of their habits, but I'd had such poor luck with the big northern variety that I was a little nervous.

I moved quietly to a spot which gave me the advantage of what wind there was, posted Way-bar, my gun-bearer, and my faithful Lu at fifteen- to twenty-yard intervals to my right, and the three outlaws at similar intervals to my left, with instructions to try and turn him back my way if he came out, and then started in after him. My youthful training under Yaqui Tom, my full-blooded Indian mentor, stood me in good stead on occasions like this, and I was wearing lightweight canvas sneakers that were the nearest things available to the moccasins I'd worn as a boy on the ranch.

I went carefully a step at a time, parting the grass and twigs with the toe of my shoe before bringing my weight down, keeping eyes peeled. Strange as it may seem I wasn't looking for a tiger but for a swarm of flies. They would mark the place where he lay with his kill. If they hovered steadily it would mean he was asleep.

If they rose and fell from time to time it would mean he was awake and swatting at them occasionally with his paw.

Suddenly I came under attack from an unexpected quarter. Small black flies resembling our American deer flies had been bothering me for some time. Now with what seemed unerring instinct they focused their attacks on my unprotected hands, face, neck, and the backs of my knees where my trousers tucked into my puttees, as if knowing perfectly well that under the circumstances I couldn't risk taking a slap at them. They fed to their hearts' content while I helplessly suffered.

I'd gone perhaps a hundred yards and had used up maybe an hour doing so, when I saw something that made me forget my painful predicament.

Thirty yards to my right was the fly swarm I'd been looking for. It was in the shadow of a tree and I'd nearly missed it and put myself upwind from a tiger. I watched it intently for perhaps half an hour. It hovered steadily. That meant he was asleep. I watched for another twenty minutes to be sure.

So far so good. But the treacherous wind was unfavorable. Should I backtrack and come around with it more in my face, or should I risk tackling him from where I stood? My flies decided me—they were literally eating me up. I couldn't stand the thought of another hour's exposure to their torture.

So I moved toward him a step at a time, keeping my eyes on *his* flies. After ten steps, they still hovered undisturbed. Ten more steps would put me practically in bed with him—if in fact he was still there. The thought ran through my mind that perhaps they were hovering over nothing but a dead pig. Perhaps he'd slipped away. Perhaps he was stalking me. I had to resist a temptation to look behind me. It was a good thing I did.

A tiger's head and shoulders had shot up in profile amid the fly swarm. Again I was looking at close range at those very orange, very black, very white markings.

I didn't contemplate them for long. His nose was up. He'd had news of me but couldn't tell just where it was coming from.

I could see the point of his shoulder as he crouched sidewise to me. As my bullet hit he went straight into the air clawing and squalling, came down and began doing backward somersaults. I had to step aside to give him room. But from the way he'd been sitting, I knew my bullet would have penetrated his heart and lungs and that he would for all practical purposes be dead before he left the ground.

He measured an inch over eleven feet from tip of nose to tip of tail. We judged his weight at 550 pounds. His skin became one of the most admired decorations of our Kalgan bungalow.

Dr. Paul S. Reinsch, American minister to China, 1913–1919, watches U.S. Marines march through the gate of the Legation Quarter, Peking.

5.

A Boy Emperor

Early in 1917 at the instigation of the International Red Cross, our American minister in Peking, Dr. Paul S. Reinsch, made arrangements with Prince Koudacheff, the Russian minister, for me to take a large camel caravan to Siberia loaded with relief supplies for German and Austrian prisoners of war held by the Russians. Dr. Reinsch's letter to his Russian counterpart may be of interest since it reveals something of the formalities of those days and the background of this particular incident.

LEGATION OF THE UNITED STATES OF AMERICA

Peking, January 26, 1917

Prince Koudacheff
Russian Minister,

My dear Colleague:

May I make known to you and bespeak your assistance in behalf of Mr. Fred M. Schroder, an American citizen who is presenting himself at your Legation to request the visa of his passport, to enable him to proceed by caravan to Kiakhta and Verchne-Udinsk and thus back to China by the Trans-Siberian Railway. The local Committee of the American Red Cross, working under the supervision of this Legation, is endeavoring to make arrangements for the transport by caravan, via Urga and Kiakhta, for a quantity of relief supplies to be delivered to the camps of prisoners of war at Troitzkosavsk, Verchne-Udinsk Park and Verchne-Udinsk Beresofka (and possibly Irkutsk and Innokentievskaia, via Baikal Lake). The arrangements for this purpose are now under consideration between the Russian Government and our Embassy at Petrograd; and if these proposals are approved, Mr. Schroder will be in charge of the caravan carrying the relief supplies.

I remain, my dear Prince Koudacheff,

Very sincerely yours,

Paul S. Reinsch

Up till now my contacts with World War I had been indirect. I knew that the Central Powers and the Allies were pressuring China to enter the war on their respective sides and were also trying (among the Allies, this was especially true of the Japanese) to enlarge their spheres of influence in China. But the U.S. by choice had no spheres of influence or special concessions and, like China, was not yet involved in the war. Events in France seemed remote and I could view with detachment some war-related incidents occurring close at hand.

The ornate lounge of the Hotel Wagons-Lits in Peking had become a center for international intrigue. At cocktail hour it resembled a scene from an old-fashioned spy movie: crowded with attachés, munitions salesmen, concession hunters, soldiers, tourists, journalists, a minister or two, gamblers, remittance men, gun smugglers, opium runners, beautiful Mata Haris, sycophants, and truly influential figures like Roy Anderson of Standard Oil. Roy—huge, fat, imperturbable, weighing nearly 300 pounds—was perhaps the most influential foreigner in all the Far East. Like Sowerby he'd been born in China of American missionary parents and knew the country and its people intimately. In his hotel room, surrounded by whiskey bottles, poker chips, and tobacco smoke, he held court like a mandarin. He was the only foreigner I knew who could outtalk an Oriental, and I've seen him sit for the better part of two days surrounded by shouting Chinese, each suggesting how, when, and where things ought to be done, while Roy slowly and certainly consumed one bottle of whiskey after another, and talked right back, and at the end of two days the whiskey was gone, the Chinamen were silent, but Roy was still talking. Hutchison liked to tell how he sat in a poker game with Roy and three high-ranking officials in a room at the Wagons-Lits and watched one of the officials gracefully lose $200,000 to the other two. Next day the loser was proclaimed head of the Peking octroi.

How you did it mattered as much or more than what you did. Form, face, were vitally important.

Roy was edging China toward the Allied side, the side of Standard Oil, Democracy, and the U.S.A.

Because of my German name and the fact I could speak their language thanks to my German uncle, and because I had certain contacts, the Germans regarded me as someone who might be useful to them and went out of their way to cultivate me. Earlier they'd invited me to visit their naval base at Tsingtao and after a bibulous weekend had presented me with a tiny white piglet as a souvenir. I took her home to Kalgan, christened her "Miss Bacon," raised her on brandy and condensed milk (there were no cows to speak of and consequently no fresh milk in China, cows being too costly to feed, and even the Mongols preferring mare's milk), and when she'd grown to weigh 200 pounds Miss Bacon would still come to the verandah at tea time for her lump of sugar.

Now I was taken by a well-known German *bon vivant*, a familiar figure at the bars of the Wagons-Lits and Peking Club, said to be the illegitimate son of the Kaiser, to an interview at the German Legation with their minister, Admiral von Hintze. An adventurer as well as statesman, Hintze was tough. He later engineered the stepping down of the Kaiser after Germany was defeated and was now famous locally for having reached China disguised as a stoker on a Swedish freighter, thus evading Allied naval ships during the long voyage from Europe. After cigars and a drink or two and a polite reference to my numerous trips into Mongolia, he asked if I knew anything about a small caravan reported to have left one of the foreign trading compounds at Kalgan a month or two earlier bound for Urga. I guessed what he was driving at and told him frankly what I'd heard.

Late one night a small caravan of twenty or thirty camels left the compound of our neighboring, German-owned trading firm, Arnhold, Karburg & Company, and took the usual route up the pass into Mongolia. Its cargo, however, was rather unusual. Instead of bricks of tea and bales of cloth it carried kegs of powder and sticks of dynamite. You couldn't keep a cargo like that secret. Long before the caravan reached wherever it may have intended to go, it was seized by a band of heavily armed Mongols. They arranged its powder kegs in a circle, stacked dynamite around the bottom of each keg and set a bound captive on top, connected everything to a single fuse, and blew the whole business to kingdom come.

"O-o-o-h!" was all Hintze said, very softly. Later I learned that the Imperial German Government had through Hintze ordered Captain Rabe von Pappenheim, its military attaché in Peking, to interrupt the heavy traffic of munitions and men on the Trans-Siberian by permanently destroying the line. Rabe, therefore, outfitted a "hunting and scientific" expedition to visit Mongolia, en route of course to Siberia. With unfortunate results.

So ended the German attempt to blow up the Lake Baikal tunnels on the Trans-Siberian Railroad. If successful it might have blocked the line for a considerable period (there were a number of tunnels bordering the lake) and significantly disrupted the movement of men and supplies from eastern Siberia and the rest of the Far East—Japanese materiel, especially—to the Eastern European battlefront where Russians and Germans were fighting.

Thanks to better advance arrangements, my caravan trip across Mongolia and into Siberia with Red Cross supplies went off without difficulty, and I delivered my cargo of clothing and food stuffs at Troitzkosavsk, Verchne-Udinsk Park, Verchne-Udinsk Beresofka, and Irkutsk for distribution to prisoner-of-war camps in those areas and returned by rail to Peking. Memories of that and other trips on the Trans-Siberian Railway and on the post roads serving it and in the towns nearby come to my mind: the way Jews in those Czarist times were spit upon on the street and any Jewish woman found in public was considered public property; the way the mujiks or peasants were treated by their superiors as slaves or dogs to be beaten or kicked at will; service on the Trans-Siberian was so poor that to make it halfway decent we used to tear a ten-rouble note in half at the beginning of a trip and hand it to the conductor. He knew that if he took care of you he'd get the other half when you reached your destination. My general impression of the Russians was one of immense good-natured strength coupled with what seemed innate lethargy and sometimes extraordinary cruelty. Speed would always beat them. But if they ever learn to be quick, watch out. In lesser degree the same was true of the Mongols. Using holds learned while wrestling with Frank Gotch at Dawson on the Yukon, I could throw Mongols who outweighed my 165 by nearly a hundred pounds. But it was largely because I was quick and knew techniques they didn't. The same was true of shooting. Russians, Mongols and Chinese were unfamiliar with the speedy accurate offhand and snap shooting techniques many of us on the western U.S. frontier had known since boyhood and had been obliged to use more than once in field conditions. Thus they were apt to be a second or two late when it counted most. As for stunt shooting, when I drew and hit coins tossed in the air, or put bullets down the necks of bottles without breaking any glass but that of the butt, they grew wide-eyed with astonishment and tended to think all Americans possessed of a little magic. But back home there were many who could shoot as well or better than I.

Back in Peking, I found it increasingly a center for intrigue. Since the death of President Yuan Shih-kai in the summer of 1916, China's political situation had deteriorated rapidly. On the one hand were liberals pushing for a more democratic government, on the other conservatives who'd backed Yuan, quite rightly it seemed to me, as the one man able to bring order out of impending chaos. Yuan was no saint but he had courageously resisted the imposition of British opium and he realized that a country ninety percent of whose people were illiterate could not become a self-governing democracy overnight as some starry-eyed liberals seemed to think. Truly he had China's best interest at heart, and now that he was dead the conservatives were talking about restoring the monarchy in the person of the boy Pu-Yi, the last Manchu emperor, who'd been deposed by the Revolution of 1911. Meanwhile, with a do-nothing parliament and an ineffective president, the country was drifting into warlordism and outright civil war.

At Peking in 1917, American volunteers, 115-strong, lined up for service in the war against Germany.

I was at Kalgan when I got a telegram which implied that something interesting was afoot. It came from W.R. (Billy) Giles, special correspondent for the Peking and Tientsin *Times* and for several American and British newspapers. He shared rent with me on a house near the Legation Quarter. Billy wanted to know if I could come to Peking immediately. I took the next train and reached our house on the Mao-chung Hutung late the afternoon of June 30, 1917. Billy was busy in his office off the living room with an interpreter and a secretary, so I poured myself a whiskey and soda at the bar in the dining room and settled onto the ottoman to relax and read the latest news. In a few minutes Billy finished his work, dismissed his help, poured himself a drink and began giving me the lowdown.

He spoke seriously; this was heavyweight stuff. Russia, having overthrown the Czar, was tottering along under the Kerensky regime, about to collapse. The Allies were preoccupied by the war in Europe. The Japanese were preparing to take advantage of the situation by seizing control of China. They'd stepped up their aggression a year or two before by presenting their infamous Twenty-One Demands and seizing all of Shantung province which had been under German control. The Allies, preoccupied then as now and anxious to keep them in the war as an ally, had let them get away with it, and so had a weakened and intimidated China. Now the Japs were planning to extend their influence. They might even seize Peking on some pretext or other. They maintained a large contingent of troops at Tientsin and could easily move them up and take the capital from the corrupt and feeble government.

"President Li Huan-hung is definitely their man," Billy asserted. "If someone doesn't stop them, they'll soon have the whole country. That's what the meeting is about tonight."

The meeting that night of June 30 had been in preparation for some time. It was held at the residence of a prominent merchant between the south and east gates. Fifty or sixty military, political, and business leaders were present. Dominant among them were the pigtailed, mustachioed old war dog Chang Hsun, who had served the Dowager Empress and been intimate with Yuan Shih-kai; and the liberal senior statesman Kang Yu-Wei, who had nearly persuaded the Imperial Government to accept reforms in pre-revolutionary days. Also present were a number of foreigners sympathetic to the republican cause, although some of them had supported Yuan Shih-kai as the only viable leader under the circumstances.

Old Chang Hsun harangued us. He'd moved a detachment of troops into the city secretly and was prepared to seize power now, tonight, and restore the Manchus to the Dragon Throne in order to establish political stability and prevent China from falling into Japanese hands. The restoration would be accompanied by creation of a constitutional monarchy patterned on England's. A national plebiscite would be held to permit the Chinese people to approve or disapprove it.

Chang proposed that, backed by his troops, we go at once to the presidential residence in the Imperial City and demand the resignation of Li Huan-hung, whom he characterized as a Japanese puppet, and then to the Winter Palace where the boy Pu-Yi, the last of the duly constituted Manchu emperors, had been held captive since the age of six when he'd been deposed, and there complete the coup d'état by restoring Pu-Yi to the throne. Pu-Yi had been painlessly deposed by the 1911 revolution and held in the palace ever since as a dangerous but valuable symbol of imperial legitimacy. Chang's most compelling arguments were that speed and secrecy were essential, that faced with a *fait accompli* the Japanese would not dare intervene, and that most Chinese—he emphasized the "most"—being weary of political instability and foreign intervention would support a traditional symbol of authority such as the boy emperor.

When Chang's proposal was supported by Kang Yu-Wei and other respected leaders, the climate in the room became such that to oppose it seemed not only bad form but unpatriotic, and it was unanimously approved.

The meeting adjourned and Billy and I went with the others to the Imperial City. Peking was divided into four cities or districts: the Chinese, the Tartar, the Imperial contained within the Tartar City, and the Forbidden City with its Winter Palace contained within the Imperial City.

The gates in the high red walls of the Imperial City were guarded by Chang Hsun's pigtailed troops so we had no difficulty gaining access. We proceeded directly to the Throne Room of the Winter Palace, learning later that President Li Huan-hung had thwarted Chang's plan to demand his resignation by fleeing and taking refuge in, appropriately, the Japanese Legation.

The Throne Room, or at least the room used for this occasion, was about forty feet by sixty, its walls covered with rich tapestries and its floor with a thick carpet of reddish ply. Electric bulbs had recently displaced the candles of the ornate chandeliers but there were still large candles in holders along the front of the dais at the end of the room where the throne or chair stood elevated, framed by gold filigree and lacquered woodwork.

The Boy Emperor in ceremonial robes of the Ch'ing Dynasty at the time of his brief restoration.

It was two in the morning when Pu-Yi appeared at the door through which we had entered, surrounded by tutors, eunuchs, and other members of his personal staff. He was a little shaver, only eleven years old, and looked rather bewildered. He wore a cap of dark blue silk, a cloth-of-gold robe richly embroidered with jewels, and a gold neck-chain.

We all stood up. Chang Hsun accompanied by Kang Yu-Wei and one or two other leaders approached the boy, bowed low, and escorted him to the dais. Before seating him on the throne, Chang made him a flowery speech in which he said that events had decreed that the future of China be placed in firm and wise hands and so the gods had recalled the Manchus to their ancient power. Coached beforehand, the boy replied that, unworthy though he was, he humbly accepted the responsibility which necessity had thrust upon him. Then Chang led him onto the dais and seated him on the throne.

The Great Seal, a device resembling those ponderous hand-stamps our American printers used to print dodgers with, was brought and placed in his lap and in a brief speech he promised always to use it wisely in the tradition of his illustrious predecessors. That was the heart of the ceremony. There was no crown, no prayer or other sacred rite. It was all over in a few minutes.

It had happened so quickly and smoothly that there seemed no reason to doubt its success—given the widespread support of the monarchical idea and the distrust of the present government and its close relationship with Japan.

Word of the coup d'état was sent immediately to the foreign legations. The influence of the foreign powers was such that no political regime was likely to succeed without their approval. They controlled about eighty percent of China's territory, most of her trade and finances including her internal customs, and their influence on her armed forces—through supplying munitions, training young officers, or bribing old ones—was enormous.

Billy went to send dispatches to his papers. I volunteered, in company with a number of other foreigners, to work with the new regime. It looked like the most interesting thing to do at the moment. Among my white colleagues was a gutty little Australian journalist named Smith who, for kicks, had climbed the outer wall of Peking with me one night when we were less sober than we should have been, wearing felt-soled Chinese shoes and wedging our fingers and toes between the cracks in the bricks to see how the smugglers did it. There was also Spurling the Sparrow. He was a former German Army officer, a large man, mechanically talented, who'd been captured by the Japanese when they seized the German base at Tsingtao and thrown into prison where he got so little to eat he said afterward he felt like a sparrow. Spurling means "sparrow" in German. Earlier he'd had charge of the Dowager Empress' gold-plated automobile and later of a small fleet of a dozen or so motor cars with which the Chinese government hoped to haul troops onto the plateau above Kalgan during the war against Mongolia. He'd also been mechanical superintendent of the "Chinese Air Corps," a handful of planes, mostly French made, located at the racetrack outside the walls of Peking where we raced our Mongol ponies and where Spurling helped us build a biplane out of piano wire, bamboo, and cloth, powered by a twelve-horsepower engine, which several of us flew until she came down one day on a sandbar in the dry streambed below Kalgan and quit. Spurling was given responsibility for helping procure munitions and other supplies for the new government's troops. I was assigned to help my old general, Wong Shih-tai, organize internal security. I'd known Wong since revolutionary days when he had supported the republican cause and served for a time on the border. We posted guards at banks and pawnshops where looting was likely to start if it started, and dispatched small bodies of cavalry to patrol the streets with instructions to keep people moving and prevent disorder.

By 4:00 A.M. on July 1 the news was out: the Manchus were restored to the throne of China as an interim measure to preserve law and order pending the establishment of a constitutional monarchy and the holding of a national plebiscite in which the Chinese could choose between a republic and a limited monarchy. The lives and property of foreigners would be respected. Business would continue as usual.

Our headquarters was established in the War Ministry Building in the Imperial City. The Imperial City surrounded by its high walls resembled the heart of Washington, D.C., in that it contained numerous administrative buildings housing various executive offices and bureaus of government. The buildings, however, were of modest size, two or three stories high at most—in fact most of Peking except for an occasional temple was composed of one-story buildings as a consequence of the old law which forbade a Chinese to have a house higher than one story lest he presume to think of rising to the level of his Manchu overlords. All of this low-rise construction was set off by central tree-lined avenues and many beautiful private gardens whose foliage rose above their walls, and by the spacious Imperial City itself which was landscaped with parks, gardens, streams, lakes, and even an artificial mountain; so that, despite many narrow and tortuous byways, the general impression of Peking was one of spaciousness and beauty.

General Wang Shih-cheng, chief of staff in the former or yesterday's regime, became chief of staff in our new one. One of Wang's first acts was to send a message to young General Li Chin Hsi, a trusted partisan of the restoration movement, who commanded a large body of troops at the strategic railroad junction of Shih-kia-chwang, which I've mentioned, some 200 miles south of Peking. Wang asked Li to move his men to Peking immediately and bring his artillery. Our military situation was precarious. Chang Hsun's detachment, combined with the Peking garrison, which had come over to our side in its entirety, totaled only about 6,000 men. We had no artillery and there were several warlord armies in north China that might turn against us, depending on how payoffs went or power plays developed, not to mention the Japanese who might try to move up in force from Tientsin.

As word of restoration spread throughout the city, yellow dragon flags, symbols of the Manchu regime, appeared on all sides as if by magic. Some of this was the usual Chinese obedience to whatever authority appeared strongest but much was genuine. Peking had always tended to support the imperial cause, as had most of China, the revolutionary liberals being stronger in the south.

Things went well throughout that first day of the coup. In the late afternoon, General Li detrained at the Chienmen Gate with the advance elements of his Shih-kia-chwang force and came in person to headquarters. He had moved with surprising speed. Like many of China's younger officers he'd been trained in Japan, Japan's victory in the Russo-Japanese War having given it much prestige in Eastern eyes. At the time of the 1911 Revolution, Li commanded troops in the western provinces and had led them into the republican camp, thus establishing his credentials for the future. He soon became a favorite with Yuan Shih-kai. I hadn't seen him for several years. He still wore a mustache but had acquired several extra pounds. He struck me as a little more dapper, suave, and sophisticated than he should have been—much more so than the older military generation represented by the rough-cut Chang Hsun, Wang Shih-cheng, and my old Wong. However he outlined his plans with a precision which left us encouraged. Within two days he would have a protective cordon of men and artillery around the city strong enough, in all likelihood, to repel any attack.

Wang's final instructions to him were not to open fire without express orders from headquarters. It was essential to keep control of an unstable situation and avoid incidents that might lead to intervention by the foreign powers, particularly the Japanese.

All went well on July 2. No word had come from Reinsch or the other ministers as to their reaction to the coup but that was understandable. They would be contacting their respective governments for instructions and waiting to see what developed before declaring themselves. We still hoped for a personal interview with Reinsch. Chang Hsun had asked for it. The U.S. position in Chinese eyes was relatively strong because we'd demanded no extraterritorial rights or other special privileges, but instead fostered an open-door policy. Chang hoped that by gaining U.S. backing he could induce other nations to follow suit and at the same time increase his popular base of support.

General Li betrayed the Restoration Movement that replaced Pu-Yi on the throne of China for twelve hectic days.

Meanwhile the million inhabitants of Peking went about their business as if nothing unusual were happening and by nightfall a substantial percentage of Li's army and some artillery were in position around the city. For the first time in three torrid summer nights (Peking in summer can be very hot) I flopped on a cot in headquarters building and got some sleep.

I was wakened in broad daylight by the roar of a shell exploding in the grounds outside our building. It brought me to my feet with the instantaneous conviction that the Japanese had slipped up from Tientsin during the night and were attacking the city, a conviction shared at first by almost everyone else at headquarters. Everything was in confusion as two or three more shells exploded in quick succession. They were three- and four-inch stuff, much larger than anything we possessed, and were being delivered with skill by someone who understood the principles of indirect fire. Then a telephone call to the main guardhouse at the Chienmen Gate (Western Electric Company had installed Peking's telephone system a few years earlier) told us the truth. Those were not Japanese shells. They were Li's. The Japs had gotten to him and he had sold us out.

I never learned exactly how it happened. Li may have been their man from the days of his early training in Japan. They used people that way, planning far ahead. It took the Chinese, for example, several centuries to weaken the warlike Mongols by fostering pacifistic Lamaism among them but it worked. Similarly Japanese plans for dominating China dated back into the 1800s but weren't fully implemented until the 1930s and '40s.

Wang sent Li a haughty message demanding to know the meaning of his shellfire. Li replied with an ultimatum: "Surrender or be destroyed." Wang retorted with an order to the traitor to lay down his arms or bear the consequences of his treason, and we got ready to fight. Our position if awkward was not hopeless. Though outnumbered ten to one and lacking artillery, we had a million people hemmed into the city with us and with their help and the assistance of friends elsewhere we might win out.

Li began by shelling the racetrack outside the walls which was held by our men. He set fire to its stables, and racehorses broke loose or were freed by their grooms and galloped wildly in all directions, adding to the confusion, while our men fell back, trading space for time, throwing up barricades, setting the pattern we would follow.

Chang Hsun had sent messages to army commanders north and south of Peking urging them to march to the aid of the government.

Next Li shelled the guardhouses over the gates, knocked them out quickly, and positioned his guns in the gates and in some cases on top of the city walls, while his men advanced along the streets. We replied as best we could with machine guns and rifles, making him pay and suffering some losses ourselves.

Civilians ducked in and out of the firing. Foreigners stood on the wall at the Legation Quarter, which backed up against the wall of the Tartar City, to observe the fighting and one or two were hit by stray bullets we learned later. Pu-Yi remained in seclusion in the recesses of the palace, issuing edicts prepared by others. Chang Hsun had been named premier of the new regime, the veteran liberal Kang Yu-Wei secretary of state.

The foreign press was screaming about an imperialist coup d'état. Rumors flew that the Germans had staged it all in order to bring China into the war on their side. The Allies were hypersensitive on this point, being engaged as I've said in an intensive effort to get China and its manpower into the war on their side, and the fact that some of us had German names lent support to the rumors of a German plot.

The restoration got a bad press generally. Most of the reporters, Giles excepted, had little idea what was going on and wrote their dispatches as usual in the Wagons-Lits bar. When Billy showed me some of the headlines later I was aghast: REACTIONARIES SEIZE CONTROL OF CHINA, GERMANS IN THE IMPERIAL PALACE, and so forth. It was pretty sickening.

On the Fourth of July, riding past the entrance to the Foreign Quarter, I was tempted to turn my horse inside past the U.S. Marine guards, join the annual Independence Day Party (complete with bunting, champagne, and a military drill on the parade ground) at the U.S. Legation—and ask Dr. Reinsch to intervene on our behalf. Reinsch was an exceptionally able minister who really understood the situation in China. He'd been on the faculty at the University of Wisconsin before coming to the Far East and had a human touch as well as brains. I felt sure he realized the seriousness of the Japanese threat but perhaps misjudged our motives. However, Americans weren't supposed to be actively involved in the coup d'état and I decided I might harm our cause by making an appearance, and so rode on.

You may ask why I got myself involved in this troubled situation. The answer is that it was my nature to do so. I think that we are attracted to what we ourselves are: like seeks like. Frans August

Larson lived a lifetime in Mongolia and once told me he'd never had to kill a man or even use violence except on one or two occasions. Larson, though strong and virile, was a man of peace. He exuded peace. He created peace wherever he went. I was much the opposite. I was attracted to conflict. And perhaps created some of it wherever I went, without deliberately intending to or knowing that I did. I'd come to China primarily for excitement and adventure. After 1906 things were quieting down in Alaska. The easy gold was gone, the fun and furor largely over. The lonely frontier which had beckoned me in 1894 was a thing of the past. The day of consolidation and bureaucracy, corporate ownership and management had set in. The new horizon for individual enterprise seemed to me the Far East where the Manchu Empire was crumbling and opportunities of many kinds for adventure and profit seemed sure to accompany the turmoil that did, as I had foreseen, follow the downfall of the Imperial Regime. But I had never planned on being present at its resurrection.

Bad news came. The armies north and south supposedly hurrying to our aid were barely moving. In the south a blown bridge halted Chang Hsun's main force. His troops detrained and started to march but their progress was hopelessly slow. In the north, General Feng Ling-ko, commander north of the Wall, rounded up most of the railroad cars in Manchuria to move men to our aid but somebody paid him off, or he got cold feet, or both. Many had cold feet to start with. Some sold out. No one came.

Our hopes of support from the foreign powers faded too. All of them except Japan maintained a hands-off policy, while the foreign press and most of the local English language papers shouted louder than ever about imperialists and reactionaries in league with German agents. They claimed we were overthrowing the legitimately constituted Chinese Republic and leading China into the war against the Allies. In the context of the times, it was effective propaganda. The repressive regimes of Manchus and Hohenzollerns could easily be linked in the public mind, and an attempt to restore the former could be made to appear an attempt to support the latter.

The Japs encouraged such false impressions and tried to persuade other powers to intervene with them against us. They failed but continued their behind-scenes efforts to undermine the restoration through bribery and intrigue.

When the coolness of the Allies became evident and no reinforcements reached us, our leaders began to disappear in what was then typical Chinese style. Their instincts for self-preservation overcame any scruples they may have had about disloyalty to their colleagues or betrayal of our cause. It was easy to change allegiance. There were no fixed battle lines. All you had to do was cross the street and mingle with the crowd or slip out of the Forbidden City and not return. Chang Hsun took refuge in the Legation Quarter, as did Kang Yu-Wei.

Our troops, by contrast, remained loyal. They'd fought well although unpaid for several months. Now they were in a fix. As prisoners they would have little to look forward to but empty stomachs or a bullet in the back of the head. Their plight, plus a conviction that our cause was the right one, persuaded me to stay on a little longer in company with a few officers and politicians who felt similarly inclined, or had no other place to go.

Li split us into two groups. Six hundred including myself took refuge in the Forbidden City. Twenty-two hundred holed up in the Temple of Heaven a mile away. There was a lull in the fighting on the eighth and ninth of July while rumors flew and negotiations went on behind the scenes. On the tenth, a French-made biplane flew over the palace and dropped two bombs that did no damage to speak of but showed that superior force, including the latest military technology, lay with our adversaries. Nevertheless we had some good cards left.

Shortly before dawn on the morning of July 12 Li made a formal demand for our surrender.

When it was refused, he attacked the Forbidden City with artillery and small arms fire. There was a sharp skirmish at the main gate in which we lost twenty to thirty men killed and wounded. By noon his people were coming over the walls on scaling ladders, virtually unopposed because we were too few to defend them in strength. Further resistance seemed futile so we asked for a parley and half a dozen of us including myself and our finance minister, Chang Chen-fang, practically the only ranking official left, went out under a flag of truce in front of the gate to talk with Li, while our men kept their rifles on him and his aides, and his men kept us similarly covered.

Street scene, Peking, July 1917

General Li's men scaled the wall of the Forbidden City to attack us during the fighting in Peking, 1917.

Since we had asked for the parley, protocol required that we speak first. Without a word Chang handed him a paper stating our armistice terms. Our men were to be paid in full, by Li. They were to be allowed to keep their arms and ammunition and return to their homes unmolested. There were to be no reprisals. A national plebiscite was to be held to determine whether China preferred a limited monarchy or a republic. And in return Pu-Yi would step down from his throne and fighting would cease.

Li scanned the paper contemptuously, then asked why he should sign such an absurd document when we, not he, were the defeated party.

"So the Foreign Legations will know what you've agreed to!" Chang replied. This caused him to glance at me.

"And if I do not choose to sign?" His voice was obnoxiously oily.

"Then you and your friends can come to power over the ruins of the palace. We won't leave one stone atop another. You can have what's left."

It was a bluff but one we could make good. We knew that destruction of the palace was the last thing he wanted. For generations it had been the focus for the ancestor worship of the entire nation. Despite the revolution, it remained dear to most Chinese. To come to power by destroying it would be a bad beginning indeed.

After much beating around the bush, including some remarks about our criminal insurgency and his praiseworthy desire to avoid further loss of life and property, Li signed the paper as though it was nothing. Actually it was rather remarkable. It represented one of the few instances where the victors not only agreed to pay the vanquished but allowed them to retain their arms. We based it on the belief that he and his Japanese masters wanted us out of the way as quickly and quietly as possible. It could perhaps have happened only in the Alice-in-Wonderland world of Chinese politics where all things are possible.

"Now, if you'll clear the way," we told him summarily, "we'll march our men to the Temple of Heaven and you can pay our combined forces there." We never let him take the initiative, kept him constantly on the defensive—for having defeated us but not yet disposed of us! He was looking rather unhappy by this time, sensing himself in danger of losing face.

By prearrangement we left the boy emperor in the palace. The less he saw of us now the better. Later he would disclaim his involvement in the coup, saying we had coerced him. Years later he would again play the role of puppet when the Japanese rehabilitated him and made him emperor of their puppet state of "Manchukuo" or Manchuria (plus parts of Inner Mongolia) during World War II.

We marched our men to the Temple of Heaven through a cordon of Li's troops. "Hold onto your arms," we instructed them. "When you've been paid, wait in the temple compound until every man has been paid. Then we'll all march out together. Be ready to fight if need be."

We didn't think Li would risk trying to kill us there at the heart of Peking with so much attention focused on him but we couldn't be sure.

The Temple of Heaven was an extraordinary structure and one of China's most sacred shrines. It was circular, three stories high, built of masonry and stone, with three tiers of blue-tile roofs, surrounded at ground level by marble balustrades and a compound. Every winter solstice, the emperor used to offer sacrifices there to the one god, Shang-ti. If anything the temple was a more sacred place than the palace. Its confines should never be defiled by violence, which was one reason our people had taken refuge there. Sharing the premises with them were a number of resident priests who officiated at the temple's shrines. They were friendly to us and had entered into our plans.

On arrival, we sent Li word that we were ready to meet him in the anteroom and implement the surrender agreement with his payoff of our troops. The anteroom was situated to one side of the temple's main entrance. It was often used by the priests to conduct business with the public. As Li and his party entered it through the main door, we did likewise through a side door opening into the compound. Again we showed our contempt by being a few steps late.

But this time when I saw him I lost my temper. The accumulated tensions and resentments of the past few days burst out. What triggered me was not so much Li as the three uniformed Japanese officers who were with him. He would be using their money to pay our men and they had come along to see he didn't cheat them. In the face of the sacrifices that had been made and the blood that had been shed, it was all so blatantly corrupt that next thing I knew I was confronting Li. Most of what I said doesn't bear repeating. But everyone there heard it.

"You sold us out," I concluded.

"I acted entirely for the good of the country!" he replied haughtily.

"*Your* good!" I said. "Good of the country hell! I know you got your dollars for it. You sold the country to the Japs, Li."

"I'll have your head," he said, smiling that conventional smile with which they can bless or kill you.

"It's waiting for you to come and take it," I replied.

I watched him redden. His loss of face would be irreparable so long as I lived.

I laughed at him. I was wearing pistols in open holsters and I think he realized I could use them before he or his men could stop me. He was also still uncertain as to what power interests I represented and I guessed that this would help restrain him until he could find just the right moment to retaliate.

We sat down across the table from each other, among our respective groups, and my men began to file in from the temple compound while his clerks and our paymasters paid them—two dollars per man per month in the average case—and the Japanese officers watched to see there was no cheating.

The payoff took most of the day and caused considerable unrest among Li's troops because they hadn't been paid. The Japs were investing all they could afford for the moment in us, not in his overdue bills. Eighty-thousand dollars borrowed from the Yokahoma Species Bank was a figure commonly given for the payoff. All of this came out in the newspapers and later in magazines and books but surprisingly little was made of it. When the restlessness of his people became apparent we smiled and joked about it. That was the last straw. It really galled Li. "Your turn will come!" I could see him thinking when he glanced my way. Finally the last of our boys was being paid and I knew my turn had indeed come.

The ruse I'd decided to use was time-worn but seemed the best available. Keeping my eyes fixed on Li, I stood up, stretched my arms deliberately, and said I was going to go to the toilet, having been sitting at that table most of the day. Then I turned my back on him and began walking slowly toward the door which led from the anteroom into the main part of the temple. He could have stopped me. Perhaps he thought me trapped. His men filled the anteroom and compound outside. A mouse would have had a hard time getting through them unnoticed, let alone a white foreign devil. In any event he did nothing.

Quickening my pace I passed through the central shrine where the punk sticks were burning and the statues of the gods sat roundabout and descended a flight of steps that led to a corridor, glancing back now and then to see if I were being followed.

At the end of the corridor was a toilet room where the honey pots stood open in rows at either side, exuding their unforgettable aromas, and as I reached it I saw with intense relief that the wooden door at the far end of it was unbarred. Another moment and I was safe in the living quarters of the priests beyond.

I dropped the bar into place on that side, and it didn't take long to change my clothes. I kept my long-handled underwear and .45s as foundation garments. Outwardly I became a Buddhist priest wearing faded red robe, peaked wool cap, felt-soled shoes. Iodine added to the natural tan and dust and dirt of hands and face. The humor of it began to sink into me along with the iodine and for the first time in a week I began to enjoy myself. Then I joined a religious procession that was forming. Carrying paper banners and intoning prayers, we priests marched up the ramp into the temple compound and out the gate, passing through Li's men and a number of my own, who weren't looking for me in such pious company.

A quarter of a mile into the city and four or five of us turned off along a side street to a small temple where a rickshaw was waiting. By now I was having a ball. Usually it took an hour to cross Peking by rickshaw. It took me about thirty minutes. When one boy tired, another replaced him. They knew the shortcuts and shouted at the top of their lungs whenever traffic blocked our way. To onlookers I was simply a priest in a hurry.

At the North Gate ten or twelve of my Kalgan riflemen—soldiers who lived in Kalgan and who carried the rifles and ammunition with which they had left the Temple of Heaven despite orders to the contrary—were waiting for a train to take them home. The sight of them gave me an idea. A locomotive with steam up and a boxcar attached was standing on the track heading up the line. Whether it had been arranged for or not I didn't know but we didn't stop to ask. The engineer and fireman were at first paralyzed with amazement when a red-robed priest presented a pistol at their heads but soon became cooperative. We uncoupled the car. I rode in the cab. My boys swarmed onto the tender.

From Kalgan I proceeded on horseback to the Mongolian Plateau. There I tapped the telegraph line and sent a message to Li, which he almost certainly never got, saying that if he would come alone to the top of the pass I would meet him there alone and we could settle our differences.

Within a few days, reports reached me that he'd placed a price on my head. To be on the safe side, I spent the next few months in Mongolia.

The restoration failed through lack of planning and good luck. It wasn't an unscrupulous power grab but a sincere attempt to save China from falling into Japanese hands. Chang Hsun was sincere. His chief error lay in acting too hastily and relying on supposed friends who failed him. With better preparation and judgment, the coup could have succeeded since popular support for it was unquestionably strong. Some said later that General Tuan Ch'i-jui coming up with an army from Tientsin backed by the Japanese doomed the restoration but Li's treachery was fundamental. He set a pattern.

The abortive coup d'état was followed by what had preceded it: political chaos and Japanese encroachment. China entered World War I on the side of the Allies largely to secure herself a seat at the peace table from which she could and did protest Japan's aggression against her sovereignty. But her fragile political structure soon gave way. She was primarily a people, not a nation. She succumbed to warlordism complicated by Communism. Among the students in those early anti-government demonstrations was one named Mao Tse-tung and one named Chou En-lai. Not till the strongest of the warlords, Chiang Kai-shek, brought order in 1928 was there anything resembling peace and unification and it was soon broken by the Japanese conquest of Manchuria and Inner Mongolia in the 1930s and Japan's subsequent attempt to subjugate all China during World War II. Then in 1949 came Chairman Mao.

The boy Pu-Yi survived as I've said to become the puppet emperor of Japanese-controlled "Manchukuo" in northeast China during the 1930s and '40s. He was captured by the Russians toward the end of World War II and held prisoner by them until around 1950 when he was handed over to the Chinese Communists. At first they imprisoned him, or so the papers said. But he was later released and allowed to live in only tacit captivity while doing research in Chinese history. Poor kid. I felt sorry for him. He was always the figurehead, puppet first to last. And the last of the Manchus.

In retrospect I'm convinced that as a price for Japan's continued participation in World War I, the Allies turned their backs on the restoration of Pu-Yi. Thus they lost a precious opportunity to stabilize China and help her become democratic in a gradual way. Instead, Japan's increasingly flagrant aggressions in the 1917–1920 period turned many young Chinese such as Mao and Chou into revolutionary Communists, thus decisively changing the course of history. They saw in Japanese arrogance the culmination of foreign domination and bigotry which had been going on for decades, and their resentment found form in their revolutionary program which essentially was "China for the Chinese."

Frederick Russell Burnham, my old friend from Klondike and Southern California days, makes a statement in his book *Scouting on Two Continents* which expresses exactly the underlying feeling I sensed in China, a feeling which gave rise to much that has happened there since. Burnham who served with distinction as a scout against the Apaches in Arizona and the Matabele in Rhodesia was visiting Egypt where he fell into conversation with an old Bedouin. They were standing atop the great pyramid looking down on the khaki tents of British soldiers and the red coats moving in perfect array across the sandy parade ground. Burnham said to the old Arab: "You who are so proud—how do you feel toward the Unbeliever with the strange eyes and uncouth ways who rules over you?"

After a moment of silence the Arab replied: "For our sins Allah has seen fit to punish us by setting the foreigner over us. When in his judgment we have paid, we shall rule again. the English came yesterday. They are here today; they will be gone tomorrow. We were here before they were known. We shall be here when they are forgotten."

No Chinese ever said it to me exactly in those words but that was what their attitude implied. We foreigners with our pomp and circumstance and newfangled ways were no more than passing clouds.

Perhaps the most revealing event of the restoration was what happened on the night of June 30, 1917, when President Li Huan-hung took refuge in the Japanese Legation. When a Chinese president takes refuge in a Japanese Legation, you can be sure there is something amiss.

As for General Li, he eventually fell from favor and lost his head. So far I still have mine.

Slightly squiffed, O. Mamen (left) and I celebrate after being awarded–and wearing–China's Order of the Golden Harvest, Second Class.

6.

Farewell

I WAS witnessing the last of the old China, the first of the new. Those disturbances around the parliament building in Peking were only the beginning. With the emperor gone there was no center any more, no symbol of authority to which people could look. And we on the border, too, did not know exactly where we stood. Were the Japanese to be our new masters? Or would it be the Red Russians moving down into Mongolia from the north, taking over Urga and hungry for more?

Perhaps it was this feeling of uncertainty that led me into an accident which determined my future. I lost my snow goggles during a caravan trip in an April blizzard and the resulting snow blindness permanently impaired my sight. When the doctors in Shanghai could do little for me, it set me thinking. "You can't troubleshoot with bad eyes," I finally decided. A certain girl was waiting in San Francisco. So was our dream of a California orange ranch. Though my account at the Hong Kong and Shanghai Bank wasn't as big as it might have been, it was probably big enough.

Like China herself the old gang at Kalgan was breaking up, anyway. Brodie had headed for New Zealand, William Ashley Anderson back to the States. Brodie became one of the leading businessmen of Wellington and for a wedding gift I sent him and his wife the skin of a snow leopard picked up in that high country west of Kumbum where we'd once crossed the passes over the Kunluns into Sinkiang. After a distinguished career as author and editor, Anderson was last heard from on the Trans-Siberian viewing our old haunts from a train window en route to Australia where his daughter was married to Sir John Buchan, not he of *The Thirty-Nine Steps* but a cousin.

Oscar Mamen was last heard from leading Mongol guerillas against invading Japanese soldiers during World War II. Mamen survived, only to die tragically in an auto accident in Kenya years later while searching for new frontiers in which to adventure.

J.A. Thomas retired to his estate at White Plains, New York. There, married to a beautiful younger woman, surrounded by a magnificent collection of rare jade, he lived out his last years like the mandarin he in many respects was.

Roy Chapman Andrews was little known when he first came to our billet at Kalgan but a few years later he became world famous thanks to his caravan trips across the Gobi, as he called it—though you do not cross the true Gobi on your way from Kalgan to Urga—and his collections of fossils for the American Museum of Natural History. Andrews' books, like Larson's *Duke of Mongolia*, give the best insight I know into the Mongolia of the 1920s with its Chinese encroachments and Soviet disruption and intrigue.

Frans August Larson like Mamen hung on at Kalgan until the bitter end. One night after Larson had gone to bed his loyal Mongols came to his room and warned him the Japanese were planning to take him prisoner next morning. He left at once and eventually made his way to California where we resumed contact.

The railroad which Herbert Hoover scouted the route for on horseback between Kalgan and Urga, where he met the Living God, was eventually built. But by that time Mongolia had ceased to exist as a nation. Its northern or outer portion passed into the Soviet orbit as "Outer Mongolia." Urga became Ulan Bator or "the Red Warrior." Inner Mongolia became part of China. At the border between Outer and Inner Mongolia, near one of the wells where we used to water our camels, through traffic on the railroad is interrupted while papers are checked and the guns of the Russian and Chinese border defenses begin.

China, the world's most populous country with the world's oldest continuous civilization will, I think, emerge from its current turmoils to be again a leading nation. It has the natural resources and above all the people. Despite all the Chinese may go through, they have the inborn confidence of ages of survival. They know who they are. Who else can compare with them in terms of illustrious achievement over four thousand years?

As I stood on the deck of the Dollar liner watching the Shanghai docks recede against a twilight sky, I was sorry to leave. It wasn't so much the tall buildings and the bustle of the Bund my eyes were seeing as those wide-open spaces of the Mongolian grassland where a man might ride all his life and never see a piece of plowed ground or a telegraph pole. I was thinking of Malunga, of Wong, of Mu-Yan and my days and nights on the caravan trail, those dung fires, those meals of boiled millet and sheep and strong black tea that may corrode the stomach but warms the spirit—and the satisfaction which comes only from shared hardship and risk, and destinations reached at last.

Author's Note

IT SEEMS appropriate to add a few words about some of the subjects touched on by Schroder: first the royal tombs of Sian.

Since Schroder's time there, access to the Sian (new spelling: Xian) region by foreigners has been severely limited, first by the turmoil of civil wars, then by World War II, then by the struggle between Communists and Nationalists which followed, later by the restrictive policies of the Mao Tse-tung government. However in 1973 as part of the new openness a group of American archaeologists and art historians visited Sian under government auspices. There they saw and photographed numerous pyramidal shaped burial mounds of enormous size. And in 1975 the Peking government announced the discovery of a burial pit associated with the tomb of China's first sovereign emperor Ch'in Shi Huang Ti (d. 210 B.C.) near Sian. The pit occupied an area of several acres. Among the first relics uncovered were 530 lifesize terra-cotta warriors. These helmeted and armored figures drawn up in battle array, stood nearly six feet tall and carried real bows and arrows or held real swords, spear, and crossbows. Interspersed among them were actual war chariots each drawn by four lifesize horses. In addition many iron farm tools, gold, jade and bone objects, as well as linen, silk fabrics, leather, and wooden vehicles were discovered.

Writing in the *National Geographic* in 1978 Audrey Topping gave the first full account in English of the incredible tomb of Ch'in Shih Huang Ti, which some authorities consider the greatest archaeological find of our time. Topping vividly recalls her first view of the Sian archaeological excavations in the introduction to this book. The tomb's guardian army may number as many as 7,500 lifesize men and horses. No two of the human figures are alike and some experts think they may be actual replicas of the emperor's honor guard. The horses that stand four abreast before their royal war chariots, have their tails knotted at half length, their ears cocked forward, alert and ready to march.

Nearby an unexcavated burial mound or earthern pyramid known as Mount Li resembles a natural mountain fifteen stories high overgrown with trees. It may contain the imperial sarcophagus and its treasures may match the tomb of Egypt's Tutankhamun in riches, but it was probably entered and looted shortly after the emperor's death.

In 1978 a visiting American art historian, Professor James Cahill of the University of California at Berkeley, showed a copy of the aerial photograph of the big flat-topped pyramid which appears in this book to the experts at the Sian excavations. They could not identify the pyramid. However, Professor Te-k'un Cheng of Cambridge University, a leading authority on Chinese archaeology, identifies it positively as one of the tombs of the Han Emperors (202 B.C.–220 A.D.), successors to Ch'in Shih Huang Ti. These are situated northwest of Sian in the region where Schroder reported those he saw. "There are ten or eleven mounds in the area," says Professor Cheng, "and most have flat tops like the one in the photograph." But he adds that their dimensions are much smaller than those given for the one pictured.

But could the pyramid in the photograph be a relatively small Han tomb? Expert analysis reveals it to be about 1,500 feet square at its base and probably 500 feet or more high. (By comparison, the Great Pyramid of Egypt, also flat topped, is 450 feet high and approximately 455 feet square at its base.) Could a structure of such size as the big Sian pyramid remain unknown, or at least unpublicized, somewhere in China?

In 1908 the American Robert Sterling Clark and the Englishman Arthur de Carle Sowerby saw a burial mound so large they mistook it for a small mountain near Chung-pu Hsien, some hundred miles northeast of Sian. Current copies of U.S. Defense Department Joint Operations Map NI-49-51, Series 1501, Sheet NI 49-5, Edition I, published in 1968 by the U.S. Army Topographic Command show fifteen "pyramids" in the vicinity of Sian.

Perhaps among the amazing things yet to be discovered, or rediscovered, in China is a flat-topped pyramid of extraordinary size.

The monastery at Kumbum was not accessible to foreign visitors at the time of this writing but its sacred tree is reported alive. But how does one account for its lama clairvoyants of an earlier time? Can we accept what not only Schroder but other visitors to Tibet and Kumbum claimed to have witnessed? And many statements of scholars and yogis before and since? Robert Ekvall in *Religious Observances in Tibet* explains the presence of what we call "magic" as an essential dimension of Tibetan life. Garma C.C. Chang in *Teachings of Tibetan Yoga* explains how clairvoyance and out-of-body travel and perception can be achieved through advanced practice of yoga, as does Yogi Ramacharaka in *Fourteen Lessons in Yogi Philosophy and Oriental Occultism*. There is much similar literature.

In *Psychic Discoveries Behind the Iron Curtain*, Ostrander and Schroeder discuss clairvoyance and out-of-body travel via the telepathic or "hypnotic trance" or "sleep." In this "state of telepathic hypnosis," they say, "the subjects know about events happening at a great distance from themselves." When a subject "wakes up," the trance rapidly becomes less deep and full consciousness returns in twenty to thirty seconds much as Fred Schroder noted.

In his recently published *Indian Running*, Peter Nabokov tells of the "trance running" of the Yurok Indians of northern California.

Alexandra David-Neel who lived in Tibet for many years and at Kumbum for many months visited the monastery's "College of Ritual and Magic," In her famous book *With Mystics and Magicians in Tibet (Magic and Mystery in Tibet)*, David-Neel, the first western woman to become a lama, also tells of observing instances of telepathy, mind reading, clairvoyance, trance walking or running and explains how they are accomplished through highly disciplined concentration, meditation, and breath control.

When Fred Meyer Schroder went to Kumbum few people in the western world believed in the existence of extrasensory activities and perception. Today about a tenth of all American and European psychologists are said to accept ESP as a fact. Another tenth regard it as an impossibility. The rest treat it as an open question. Evidence for its existence seems to be growing, however, as does official interest in it. Since the 1950s the Soviet government has been reported experimenting with ESP for military as well as nonmilitary purposes. As for this country, reliable reports assert that the U.S. government, nervously aware of work conducted in Russia, is beginning to worry about a Parapsychology Gap, and in the past few years has secretly spent several hundred thousand dollars in psychic phenomena research. The National Aeronautics and Space Administration has funded a Stanford Research Institute study on ESP. The Defense Department's Advance Research Projects Agency paid for a Rand Corporation translation of all Soviet literature on paranormal phenomena. The National Institute of Mental Health funded a study in dream research at the Maimonides Medical Center in New York. The Navy reportedly is entering the field and the Central Intelligence Agency is rumored to be already in it. One study is said to involve the "sensory shielding" of the U.S. President to prevent anyone from reading his mind.

Among prominent exponents of research into paranormal behavior are the laser physicists Russel Targ and Harold Puthoff of the Stanford Research Institute at Menlo Park, California. One experiment which particularly intrigued Targ and Puthoff involved what they called "remote viewing." Their chief subject was able to describe correctly randomly selected objects situated at a distance of ten miles. These included buildings, docks, roads, gardens, and such details as structural materials and colors. He was also able to describe human activities and physical and psychic quality of atmosphere at the place observed.

In subsequent experiments other subjects were able to describe scenes as much as 1,000 miles distant with astonishing accuracy. Writing in the authoritative British scientific journal *Nature*, Targ and Puthoff stated: "What these experiments in remote viewing lead us to believe is that a channel exists whereby information about a remote location can be obtained by means of an as yet unidentified perceptual modality."

As for Kumbum's Tree of Faces, William Rockhill, the American missionary explorer who saw it in the 1890s, called it a white sandalwood. But the season was winter and there were no leaves on it so he was unable to check for images or writing and saw none on the bark which in many places curled like that of a birch or cherry. He said the lamas tried to sell him dried leaves as sacred mementos but he could see no images on them.

Alexandra David-Neel saw the tree when she was living at Kumbum in the 1920s but failed to observe any images or writing; but in the 1940s a professor from Yenching University, Dr. Y.M. Mei, was mystified when he saw images and writing on the leaves and bark. With what might be called western skepticism, Dr. Mei waited like

Schroder until his lama guide's back was turned. Then he took out his pocket knife and with its blunt edge was able to produce, he claimed, a variety of markings in Chinese, Tibetan, or English on leaves and bark.

The Old Silk Road which winds past the royal tombs of Sian and which Schroder once traveled toward Kumbum is being converted into a tourist attraction by the People's Republic of China. Visitors are told how camel caravans once journeyed over it carrying spices, jade, ivory, and gold as well as silk to India and Europe and how traders from as far away as Rome came to the great city of Sian, then known as Changan or "Long Peace," which during ten dynasties (roughly from 1100 B.C. until 907 A.D.) served as China's capital and had a population of around two million.

West of Kumbum the road enters Sinkiang, China's far-far West at the very heart of Asia, a racial and cultural melting pot where Arab, Indian, Russian, Mongol and Chinese blood have mingled for centuries. Half its twelve million people are Moslems. "Here you see how East and West interacted for nearly 3,000 years, what each took and what each gave," Professor Mu Shunying, deputy director of the Sinkiang (Xinjiang, in the new spelling) Bureau of Archaeological Research was recently quoted as saying. "It was probably the most important trade route in history and for more than 2,000 years was the main link between East and West." Chinese archaeologists are excavating more than twenty lost cities buried in sand and time along its route. Schroder and his companions added a rare Anglo-American element to its history.

An ancient Jewish community at Kaifeng, some distance south of Pao-ting-fu near where Schroder saw a similar community, originated around 960 A.D. The Kaifeng Jewish community was believed to have survived down to the upheavals of World War II and the Japanese takeover of much of China, when it reportedly disappeared. However in 1980 it was found to be still in existence, its members dressing, eating and appearing in most respects to be Chinese. According to United Press International, Ai Fen Meng, a retired carpenter living in 2,000-year-old Kaifeng, remembers when Japanese soldiers burst into his home during World War II on orders from their allies, the German Nazis, and demanded if he was Jewish.

"They came to all the houses in the neighborhood," Ai said. "We were afraid. They had guns and knives. We did not say we were Jews."

Ai and several dozen other members of seven family clans are all that remain of the Kaifeng Jewish community. Their ancestors are thought to have come originally from Palestine via India and Central Asia. Over the centuries they intermarried and blended with the Chinese. Until their synagogue fell into disrepair and was leveled in 1860, they practiced their Judaism in the Chinese language. Today they no longer do so but consider themselves ethnic Jews.

The bronze knife money Schroder found in one of the buried cities of Mongolia looks like a large, slightly convex butter knife or old-fashioned envelope opener. Such money may date to the second century B.C. and probably originated in China. Silver shoes originated in the thirteenth century A.D. and were sometimes made of gold as well. Paper money was used in China for a thousand years before the Europeans adopted it during the 1600s.

As for the hairy wild men or "wild bandits" of Mongolia and northern Tibet, real or imaginary, they may be related to the snowman or yeti of the Himalayas. Travelers in Central Asia have described such creatures for many years. One comparatively recent description came from the late U.S. Supreme Court Justice William O. Douglas. Writing of a trip to Outer Mongolia in the *National Geographic* in March, 1962, Douglas said that during a journey into a wild region he saw a movement in some bushes and asked his native guide what it was. "Maybe it's Almas," the guide replied, explaining that "Almas" was the "Snowman of the Gobi," similar to the Abominable Snowman of the Himalayas, "shorter in stature than a man, fur covered and elusive." The introduction to this volume reveals the latest findings by researchers studying the hairy wild men of China.

As for the milu or Pere David's Deer, it did become extinct in China as Schroder states, but, earlier, several specimens had been acquired by Europeans and propagated in private collections, notably that of the Duke of Bedford in England. From there the species has been reintroduced into China. It may also be seen in menageries elsewhere including the San Diego, California, Wild Animal Park. Some experts think the milu was propagated in captivity in China for an incredible three thousand years after it became extinct in its wild state and thus represents an early, perhaps the first, successful attempt at captive propagation of a species whose survival is threatened in its natural habitat.

The British-American Tobacco Company, today the world's largest tobacco company, is also one of the world's largest multinational corporations with revenues of many billions. Under its new parental name of B.A.T. Industries Limited it is based in London, does business in 54 countries, has more than 150,000 employees, deals in perfumes and cosmetics as well as tobacco products, and engages in retailing and ownership of department stores, including the Saks Fifth Avenue chain. After years of being condemned by the Chinese Communists as a prime example of imperialist exploitation, B.A.T. is, ironically, once again doing business in China in a big way. In late 1979 it signed a contract with the Chinese government whereby its operations, discontinued in 1952 when the Mao Tse-tung regime took them over, will be resumed. The company will once again produce cigarettes in a Peking factory and will also give expert advice, as J.A. Thomas and his colleagues once did, on growing, grading and producing China's leaf.

There are several eyewitness accounts of the abortive attempt to restore the Manchus to the Dragon Throne which would probably have changed the course of history had it succeeded. That by Dr. Paul S. Reinsch, U.S. Minister to Peking at the time, is one of the best. While siding with the opponents of the coup, Reinsch thought it might have succeeded with better planning and military backing since popular support for it was strong in Peking and throughout north China. Reinsch notes that the remarkable payoff of the rebel troops amounted to $80 per man in some cases. Johan Gunnar Andersson, B.L. Putnam-Weale and other eyewitnesses agree with Reinsch and Schroder as to the main events of the restoration. It was also fully if unevenly reported by newpaper correspondents. But Schroder's is the only account by a participant I have come across except the rather limited and self-serving one by Chang Hsun. Quite naturally Schroder too emphasized what he considered the idealistic aims of the coup.

Pu-Yi, however, wasn't quite the last of the Manchus. His younger brother Pu-Jie was still alive as this was being written, still living within the precincts of the Palace of Perfect Harmony in the Forbidden City, not as a ruler but as a researcher in Chinese history. The 76-year-old Pu-Jie was in good health, occupying a room in a simple courtyard, calmly and politely telling interviewers he is at peace with history and has no regrets. Like his brother he was captured by the Russians during World War II and eventually handed over to the Chinese Communists. They in turn imprisoned him for a time but later released him and treated him kindly. After a personal interview with Chou En-lai, he was granted permission to do research—in the room overlooking the courtyard where the bullets flew in 1917 in the vain attempt to restore his brother, and by implication himself as his brother's immediate successor, to the Dragon Throne.

And as for Schroder, he died at the age of 95, rich in friends and memories. To his funeral came old gray veterans of Mexican border, Klondike and China days, male and female, some nearly blind, all game, as he would have said. it fell to my lot to scatter his ashes on the piney shoulder of Cuyamaca Peak in the Coast Range of Southern California overlooking the border ranch where he grew up and, yes, looking westward, too, toward the Far East where his adventurous carrer reached its climax.

—R.E.

Acknowledgements

My thanks go to William Ashley Anderson and Carl Brandt who first put me in touch with Fred Meyer Schroder.

Cleaver Jones Salbach generously transcribed many of my interviews with Schroder and many of her own. My wife Jane listened patiently to draft after draft, and read proof of the manuscript of this book which Alice Kladnik and Sandy McDonald helped us prepare.

Librarians at the Santa Barbara Public Library and the University of California at Santa Barbara helped with background material, as did Roy Chapman Andrews and Frans August Larson. I am particularly indebted to Professor James Cahill of U.C. Berkely and Professor Charles D. Weber of the University of Southern California who visited many of the royal tombs of Xian and told me much of what they found there. Professors Prudence R. Meyer and C.Y. Chen of the University of California at Santa Barbara gave helpful advice as did Dr. Wilma Fairbank of Cambridge, Massachusetts, and Professor T. K. Cheng of Cambridge University, England. Likewise Father Albert Raskin, Archivist General, Casa Generalizia, C.I.C.M., Rome; Marise Johnson of the Metropolitan Museum of Art, New York; and Waldo Ruess of Santa Barbara.

Audrey Topping, author of *The Splendors of Tibet*, provided invaluable insights which linked Schroder's experiences in China and Tibet to present conditions there and graciously provided the introduction to this volume.

I am grateful to the Bodley Head Ltd. for permission to use the photographs of the Tashi Lama and the Monastery of Kumbum from Alexandra David-Neel's book, *With Magicians and Mystics in Tibet*, and to the editors of *Outdoor Life* and of the original *True: The Man's Magazine* for permission to use material which appeared in their pages in somewhat different form.

Special thanks go to Noel Young, Ann Koepfli, Terri Wright and the staff at Capra Press whose helpful suggestions were essential.